Driven

The Life and Times

of

Stephen Fisher

by Stephen Fisher

with Shawn Smucker

Best Wishes 6/21/21
Stephen S. Fisher

Steve Fisher
34 N. Mount Hope School Rd.
Willow Street, PA 17584

Written by Stephen Fisher and Shawn Smucker
Edited by Natalie Hanemann
Cover Image by Brooke Victoria Bowlin

What I've written down in this book are my memories. This is how I remember my life, but I am eighty-nine years old, so if my memory has served me incorrectly, I apologize. All told, I had fourteen brothers and sisters, and I'm sure if you would have asked them, each would have had a different way of describing our parents, telling the story of how we grew up, or explaining what our lives were like. That's just the way families are—everyone sees things a little differently.

This is my story. This is how I remember it.

Steve Fisher
October 2020

Table of Contents

Chapter One
The Beginning

I was born in 1931, at the beginning of the Great Depression, and by the time my parents had all fifteen of their children, I was the middle child. Two of those children died when they were young, but I'll tell you more about that a little later. In the 1930s, the average new house cost around $7,000, gas was ten cents a gallon, and a new car cost $600—not that the price of a new car concerned us. We were a great big Amish family living on a farm, and I didn't know anything different from horse and buggies and plain clothes and no electricity. At least not when I was young.

This was when the Great Dust Bowl of the United States took place, with droughts and dust storms taking over the Great Plains states. Farms out there were going under, unemployment was at record highs, and the government was doing everything they could to help farmers out. But for a lot of people, it just wasn't enough.

Those droughts weren't as bad here in the east, but we never had anything extra. I grew up on an Amish farm on Paradise Lane, in Ronks, Pennsylvania, nestled in the rolling hills between the small towns of Paradise and Strasburg. It was a nice, manageable dairy farm, about eighty-five acres, with twenty-five cows that we milked by hand. Dad wasn't interested in getting one of those newfangled milking machines—not that it mattered because we didn't have the money for one, anyway. So, it was hand-milking for us, twice a day.

If you've seen an Amish house, then you know exactly what our farmhouse was like—a lot of bedrooms and a large, eat-in kitchen. We didn't have running water, so if we needed to go to the bathroom, we had to use the outhouse. This was inconvenient, but we didn't know any different.

If I remember right, there were five bedrooms upstairs and three downstairs. Mom and Dad stayed in one of the downstairs bedrooms, and I shared the largest upstairs bedroom with five of my brothers. All six of us slept in three double beds with straw mattresses, which were large sheets sewed up like bags and stuffed full of chopped-up straw.

I guess Joe was the closest to me in age—we were only thirteen months apart—but Benny was always my favorite. We spent more time together, especially later in my life when I worked for him repairing silos. But Joe was the one who ended up staying at the home farm and taking over, and he stayed in the Amish faith, so we didn't see each other that often, at least not for many years.

But when we were little, Eli, Benny, Joe, and I spent a lot of time together, mostly doing chores. As we moved into our teenage years, we all left the Amish (except Joe). Later on in life, Eli, Benny, and I had a place up in Potter County where we went every year, the three of us along with some of our friends, and we always had a good time. But when we were younger, we never had much time to do fun things together because we were always working on the farm or walking to school.

Even after Joe left the farm, he lived on a plot of ground real close to the old homeplace, and as I got older and thought back on life, I tried to go visit Joe as much as I could. He died a few years back, and I'm at the age now where there aren't that many of us left anymore. I guess that's just how it goes.

Most of my earliest memories involve doing chores. I'm not even sure how old I was, probably barely old enough to walk and talk, but we were expected to pull our own weight. With a household our size, everyone had to do their share if we were going to survive. This meant hard work and long days. There were cows to milk and take care of, chickens with eggs to gather, and a large garden to tend. Some chore always needed to be done, and we never caught up completely.

We were what you'd call subsistence farmers—we lived off of what we grew, and what we couldn't grow or raise ourselves, we bartered for. To get us through the winter, we tended to that huge garden and canned hundreds of cans of fruits and vegetables. With as many children as my parents had, we butchered one pig and one steer every fall, cut them up in strips and pieces, and canned the meat.

We used the chicken eggs to barter for what we couldn't grow—Mom or Dad would take the eggs to the local grocery store and trade them for items like flour, sugar, and yeast to make bread and pies and such. We made our own food, and it was so good.

It was a simple life, and there's nothing wrong with that. But we never had extra, and growing up, I always told myself I was going to have a different life. I didn't want to work so hard for nothing. It just seemed like we could never get ahead, and I wanted something else.

Chapter Two
Hard Days

I don't remember this story myself because it happened soon after I was born, but I've heard it many times. I had a brother who was around two years old at the time, so I guess this was in 1933 or thereabouts. He had just learned to walk and toddle around, and one morning my dad headed to the field out back to do some work, and my brother decided he would go out and watch. So, he walked out the long lane toward the fields, trying to catch up.

A lot of us boys did that for most of our childhood— followed Dad around, wanted him to talk to us, tried to get his attention. But it never really worked. My dad didn't have any kind of a nurturing spirit, and it wasn't in him to pay us attention. I've always wondered about that, why he was so quiet, why he went about his life so much of the time as if we didn't exist.

Anyway, this was in July and the wheat was high, ready to be harvested, and the sun was hot. Well, that little boy, my brother, went missing, and the whole neighborhood turned out to look for him, calling his name, wandering all around the countryside, wading through the crops. I guess it was my older brother Jess who found him, laying in the wheat field, nearly dead from heat stroke. That little guy had taken ten or twelve steps into that wheat, and it was taller than he was, and I guess he got lost in there. It's a terrible thing to think about. When they found him, he was passed out, and not too long after that he got pneumonia from it, and he died.

Life can be sad. Those were hard days. I was just a baby, so I don't remember it happening, but I was born into that family, and so I guess it affected me. I know it affected my parents.

It was during that same year that my mom's sister's son, my cousin, was working for my dad on the farm. He was around twenty years old, and they were hanging tobacco in the barn. I guess he had climbed up on one of the rafters while they were working, lost his balance, fell to the barn floor, broke his neck, and died. Two tragedies in the same summer. Life was hard back then.

Like I said, I wasn't even a toddler at the time, so I don't remember that summer, and I can't even imagine what my mother went through. She had a baby, then, eight days later, lost a toddler, and before much time had passed, she lost a nephew in an accident on her own farm.

Sometimes life will take you into some dark places.

From what I'm told, my mother ended up spending a lot of time in the back room of the house during those years, not saying much, rarely coming out. She stayed in there, recuperating from childbirth, probably battling severe depression, and people came in to help take care of the children—friends and relatives and people who knew the family. I know my older sister Katie helped, and I'm sure the other older siblings did as well. Everyone had to pitch in. Mom wasn't well.

In the following years, the babies kept coming, and the other kids were expected to care for them. My mother bore fifteen children in twenty years without a single set of twins to space those pregnancies apart—it doesn't seem fair, but that's the way they did it back then. And two were lost.

I'm not sure what kind of a life that was for her. I did see her smile from time to time, and we did connect every so often, I guess in the way that a mother and son can. But most of what I remember of her is sadness and quiet. And absence, when she was in her room, not coming out.

Chapter Three
At the Feet of My Father

As I grew older—I'm not sure at exactly what age but I was still young—I realized that my father wasn't a talker. He just didn't communicate with us kids. I hate to say it, but it's the truth. The fact is, during my growing-up years, I never once had a conversation with my dad, and with all the work us kids did—and it was plenty—he never once told any of us, "Good job," or, "Thanks." At least not that I ever heard.

Not once.

Not one long conversation.

Not one compliment.

Never.

Actually, I never saw him show any passion about anything at all. He just didn't talk, not to anyone, and he went about his work in almost complete silence, unless he needed to correct us. I would hear him talking to my mom from time to time, but besides that, he lived inside his head. I didn't question it at the time—that's just the way it was. But when I got older, later in my teen years and in my twenties, I started to realize what I had missed out on. And I wondered what it would be like to have a father who actually spoke to you. Maybe this is why I became the kind of father I became. I don't know. It very well could be.

When I say this stuff, when it gets written out, my one aim is to tell it like it is. I don't know—maybe some won't like it, but I'm still going to tell it how I remember it. My children and grandchildren need to know these things. And maybe someone will read this and realize how important it is to talk to their children, to be tender with them, to take an interest in them and encourage them.

Like all of us, I'm sure he was the way he was because of his own growing-up years. His own father struggled with depression and was most likely bipolar (though those things weren't diagnosed in those days). His father, my paternal grandfather, would sometimes just up and leave, simply vanish without telling anyone where he was going, what he was doing, or when he was coming home. I'm sure this had a lot to do with my dad ending up a quiet person, not really talking to us, not showing much in the way of affection or excitement at life. It couldn't have been easy for him as a child, having an unstable parent, never knowing if he would wake up one morning and find his father gone, for who knows how long.

I have a memory of when I was very small, just a little kid, probably soon after I started walking. My dad, in the evening, he used to sit in the kitchen in this chair that we had, and he would read. I guess maybe the newspaper or the Bible or some other book. I don't know. I remember sitting there as a child, on the floor, and looking up at him, studying his face, watching his hands move the pages, wishing he'd acknowledge me or pick me up and put me in his lap. I wondered what that would be like.

But he never did. I just sat there on the kitchen floor, and I guess once I got to a certain age, I stopped wishing he would do that. And I stopped sitting there looking up at him.

When I raised my four children, it was different. I didn't want them to have the same experience. I made sure I communicated with them, and they have always been really delightful kids to me. There was nothing I liked better, when they were small, than coming home from work and sitting in the love seat with them, a kid on each side and a dog in my lap. I loved it when I'd get home from work and tell them I was too tired to move, and they would help me untie my boots and pull them off, one at a time. We ate dinner together every night—that was very important to me.

I guess I wanted things to be different.

I never knew much about Dad's parents, but I do remember Mom's father, Isaac Fisher. He lived in Soudersburg, Pennsylvania and was an industrious man. He was around six-two, very astute and matter-of-fact, and he sometimes came around the house when I was a little kid and worked on the farm. For some reason, he and I hit it off, so I would trail around with him while he did odd jobs.

He had a thrashing rig, orchards, and owned four or five farms. He was always a very good money manager, knew how to make money and what to do with it when he got it. He was the one who bought the old homeplace back in the late 30s or early 40s, for around $15,000, and then in the late 40s he sold it to my dad for $45,000, and that's how my dad ended up owning that farm. He paid off the debt with tobacco checks.

Isaac Fisher's wife died young, when she was in her sixties. I don't remember much about her. But Isaac was an important influence in my life, and I think many of the conversations I had with him could have been what woke me up to entrepreneurship and being a business man. He was one of the first successful people I knew, and I think I wanted to be like him.

Chapter Four
The Rotten Tooth

Growing up as we did, without much money, going to the dentist was a luxury reserved for only the worst toothaches. We just didn't have the money to go to the dentist for cleanings. It wasn't even a thought.

And by the time those toothaches got bad enough, I guess there wasn't much point in going to the dentist anymore, so Dad would take us straight to the doctor. I remember one of these times, when he took Joe and me. We climbed into the buggy and drove to Dr. Brackbill in nearby Paradise, the pain in my tooth aching with each bump of those hard, buggy wheels. I was in agony. I don't remember why Joe was there with us. Maybe he had a rotten tooth that needed to go, too.

Well, we got there eventually and the doctor pried open

my mouth and peered in, rooting around with his finger until he figured out which was the offending tooth. Oh, it hurt so bad when he pressed on it! Then, the doctor reached back into his cupboard and pulled out a bottle of whiskey, dipped his finger in it, and rubbed all around the base of the tooth. He did this a few times, numbing it as best he could.

I closed my eyes tight. I didn't want to see him reach back for the pliers or put them into my mouth. Soon enough, I felt him pushing around in my mouth, getting a good grip on the tooth. When the pliers bumped the tooth, it sent pain shooting back my jaw, and once he started pulling he wasn't going to stop.

"Hold still, boy."

There was a scratching, grating sound, and it wrenched free. I could taste the blood in the back of my throat. He packed the empty hole with gauze. He must have done the same to Joe.

"What do I owe you?" my father asked reluctantly.

The doctor seemed to think about it for a minute, then said quietly, "One dollar ought to do it."

Dad rooted around in his deep pockets, found four quarters, and laid them on the counter. I remember staring at those shiny, silver quarters. One dollar could get you a lot of things back in those days. I'm sure my dad was thinking about all he could buy with a dollar, all of which would have been worth more to him than those two rotten teeth on the counter.

Dad must have also thought a dollar was a little steep. I heard him mumbling to himself as we walked out, "Well, that was a lot of money for five minutes' work."

I didn't have the opportunity to start going to the dentist on a regular basis until years and years later, when I started working for myself. Of course, by then I needed a lot of major work—bridges and implants and the like. I did it when I could, with my own money. It cost more than a dollar, but it was worth it.

Chapter Five
Hired Out

Around that time, when I was seven or eight years old, I was given the responsibility of plowing the fields. We had a one-row walking plow, and you had to walk along behind it and the two horses pulling it. Plowing a field, one row at a time, back and forth, back and forth, was a lot of walking. It was tiring, dusty work. And it took absolutely forever.

During that time, our next-door neighbor, a farmer who wasn't Amish, owned a Farmall M tractor that pulled a three-bottom plow, and he turned over as much field in an hour as I did in a day. What took me eight or ten hours, he could do in sixty minutes. Even at the age of eight years old, I glanced over at him behind his big fancy tractor and I thought, *There is something wrong here. What am I doing, taking all day to plow with these horses and one-row plow? I'm not going to do this for my whole life. I'm not going to stay Amish when I get older.*

That's probably when the thought first entered my mind, and it kind of stuck there.

I'm not going to stay Amish when I get older.

Fast-forward a couple more years, and I was plowing again, feeling pretty bitter about the whole thing, when the plow hit a rock and the handle flew over and hit me, knocked me over, and just about broke my ribs. It stunned me for a moment, and I just sat there. The horses stopped. I could barely breathe.

I guess I had quite the temper at the time, because once I caught my breath, I hopped up and stomped over to the horse. I was going to sock him a good one . . . not that it was his fault, but I was mad, and someone had to take the brunt of it. I took a swing at that horse, and just as I did, he turned his head, and, instead of landing on his snoot, my hand crashed into that curved bit, and I nearly broke my fingers.

I turned around, sat down in the middle of the field, and cried.

I wasn't even ten years old yet, and already I was tired of being Amish.

When I was eleven, my dad started hiring me out to neighboring farms to help bring in money for the family. It was a pretty common practice in the 30s and 40s, especially for big families who didn't need the help of all of their children on their home farm. Plus, hiring me out meant one less mouth to feed, and I made money that was sent back to my dad every week. We were in a real struggle in those days—we didn't have much of anything. I would be paid twenty dollars a month, and every penny went straight to my dad. That was quite a help to the family, financially speaking. Those of us who were old enough would leave for our assigned farm on April 1, and unless the farms were very close, we would live at those farms through the summer.

When I see eleven-year-old kids nowadays and think about the kind of work I was expected to do back when I was eleven, well, it's almost unbelievable. Eleven seems far too young to be sent away from home for so long, to be given that kind of responsibility. But it was our way of life, and it was accepted.

During that first summer, I worked for Joel King on route 741, and I stayed at his house that entire spring and summer. He had two children—they were both younger than me, around five or six years old. During my time there, I woke up at 4:30 every morning, helped with the early chores, then walked to school. After school, I walked back to his farm, helped with the evening chores, ate dinner, and went to bed. During the summer, when school was out, I worked for him all day around the farm, sometimes with set chores that I did every day and sometimes with odd jobs that came up from time to time.

Being away from my family full time for the first time in my life, I cried myself to sleep every single night. And because my nerves were on edge, I also wet the bed every night. I was so ashamed of it, but there was nothing I could do to stop it. I always made sure I went to the bathroom before bed, and every morning I woke up with wet clothes and sheets.

They decided that since I was wetting the bed, I shouldn't drink anything at dinner, so they didn't give me any water at night.

Of course, after a long day of working on the farm, I was always very thirsty, but that didn't matter—no water for me at dinner time.

I wet the bed anyway.

Soon after I started working there, the strawberries were ripe, and I ate my weight in that delicious fruit. It was the highlight of the summer. But soon after that, I got boils, and they blamed the boils on my strawberry eating and wouldn't give me any more. Those strawberries were the only bright spot in my whole life at that point, and I was so sad when they wouldn't let me eat them.

I was about as sad and miserable with life as any eleven-year-old could be. I was working for someone I didn't know well, missing my brothers and sisters, and homesick. I wasn't allowed water at night before bed, and I couldn't eat strawberries. I would have done just about anything to go home.

This was in the early 1940s. The world was an uncertain place, not that I was aware of anything beyond the farm where I worked. But out there, far beyond the borders of our small Amish district, World War II was waging, the country was trying to recover from the Great Depression. Anne Frank received a diary for her birthday in 1942. The Germans had begun exterminating the Jews. The United States had begun their attempts at building a nuclear bomb.

And there I was, Stephen Fisher, eleven years old, working hard and homesick.

Then, a bright spot. In those days, the women often had quilting bees, where they would gather together and work on sewing projects. The wife of the farmer I was working for was invited to my parents' home for a quilting bee that very weekend.

I was out in the field when the farmer came to me with the much-needed good news.

"If you do a good job," he said gruffly, "I'll let you go to your house with my wife for the quilting bee tomorrow. You can see your folks and say hello. But only if you work hard today."

I worked my fanny off, looking over my shoulder all day to make sure he was watching and aware of just how hard I was working. I pulled more weeds that day than I ever had before. Oh, I was so hopeful!

And he let me go.

I got to spend all day at home with my brothers and sisters, back in that familiar house that I suddenly loved much more than I remembered, and it was such a wonderful thing. I don't know what we did that day—it probably didn't even matter. I was just happy to be home. In fact, when it came time to go back to the farmer's house, I felt sick to my stomach. I did not want to go back there. I didn't understand why my dad wouldn't let me stay. Couldn't he see how much I hated leaving? Couldn't we figure out how to make it work with me at home? I knew I'd work harder if he'd let me stay.

I slipped out into the field and hid in a shock of wheat. I stayed there, silent and still as could be, for a very long time. When it came time to leave, I could hear the voices of the people who were looking for me.

I didn't think of it at the time, but I wonder if that search caused my mother great distress. After all, just over ten years earlier they had searched the same fields for my brother, and they had found him nearly dead, lying in the field. I wonder if she was worried, or if she knew that I was hiding.

19

Everyone searched for me for a long time. So long, in fact, that the farmer's wife gave up and returned home in her buggy without me. And still I waited, hidden in that shock of wheat, taking my chances. I didn't want to leave. I wondered maybe if I could stay there, hidden for a few days, take food from my house when no one was looking. Eventually I could go back to the house and if I waited long enough, the farmer would have found someone else to work for him, and I could stay at home.

But, within a few hours, my dad found me.

He was angry, but even in the face of his anger, I still didn't want to go back.

"Start walking," he said quietly, and I knew he meant that I should start walking back to the farmer's house, which was a few miles away. I also knew that I didn't have a choice, so I started walking back toward the farm where I was supposed to be staying and working.

At some point during the journey, when Dad saw that I had resolved to go back, he turned around and let me continue through the dark on my own. I got as far as my parents' neighbor's house, went into their washhouse, and sat on the wall, crying. I just didn't want to go back in that house, because if I did, there would be no going back home—I'd be stuck there for the rest of the summer. Again, I started weighing my options, wondering if I could run away or hide out somewhere.

Well, lo and behold, I looked up and there stood my dad in the doorway of the washhouse. He had followed me across the field to make sure I kept walking.

He picked me up by the shoulders, carried me outside the washhouse, and put me down on my feet.

"Now, you walk," he said.

I had to. I didn't have any other place to go. I went back into the farmhouse and spent the rest of the summer working there. And I hated every minute of it, and I cried myself to sleep every night.

Thinking back on those days makes me really sad. I hate that my eleven-year-old self had to go through something like that, had to lose that sense of being at home, had to grow up so quickly.

I worked there that summer, and then the next summer my brother Benny was chosen to go to that farm. Well, he was there for two months before he'd had enough, and when he told one of his buddies that he wasn't going to stay, his friend had an interesting idea.

"Let's go to Florida," his friend suggested.

So, they did. Or at least they started for Florida. They got as far as Steelville before they ran out of food and ran out of money and had to ask a farmer if they could work for food. I guess they were around sixteen years old, and when the farmer saw those two strapping young men, I'm sure he thought he had hit the jackpot, so he put them up in his barn and fed them in exchange for them working for him, mostly hauling manure from the dairy barn out to the fields.

In the meantime, the farmer Benny was supposed to be working for, the same one I ran away from the previous summer, told my dad Benny was gone, and they didn't know where he was. I have no idea how they did it—in those days there were no cell phones and people weren't nearly as connected as they are today—but they found him a few days later, still down in Steelville, still hauling manure for this farmer.

When they got home, and my dad told him he needed to go back to the farmer's house, my brother shook his head.

"I'm not going back," he said. Benny was a little older than me, and I guess when he made that decision not to go, there wasn't anything my parents could really do about it.

I was getting close to that age, too, where I could make my own decisions about what I was going to do with my life. And believe me, I had some plans. And they certainly didn't involve staying Amish.

Chapter Six
Some Things, You'll Never Know

When I was in grade school, I remember there was a trolley that went from Lemon Place to Lancaster, and the tracks went right up the middle of Route 30. The guy who ran the trolley ended up being a member of our hunting camp in Potter County that we built in the late 50s. You could go to all kinds of different places on that trolley, and if you wanted to go all the way into Lancaster, it cost ten cents. It took you right into the square.

If you were in a car, you had to be careful passing in the middle lane in those days because the trolley tracks were in the center lane. Later on, they did away with the rails and turned it into a three-lane highway. This was when the buses sort of took over.

But in those trolley days, you could take it all the way from

Paradise to Lancaster and only see one or two cars, at the most. There just weren't many cars in our part of the country, and the trolley was a wonderful way to get into the city.

My brother Joe told me later in life that Dad attended the Ronks Elementary School at the crossroads. Joe said that Dad told him that when he was in school, the ships came over from Europe carrying huge loads of cobblestones in the keel. Actually, streets from Philadelphia to Harrisburg were made using those cobblestones, and this meant that when a car traveled up Route 30, you could hear them thumping along on the cobblestones.

My dad's teacher would say, "I think I hear a car coming!" and everyone would rush to the window or out onto the porch, just to watch the car go by.

My dad and I traveled into the city on the trolley one day, and it was my first time in the big city of Lancaster. I'm not sure if I was even old enough to be in school. It was very rare that my dad ever went into the city—I can't even remember what our mission was on that particular day, but for some reason he brought me along with him.

Once the trolley arrived in the city, click-clacking along the track, occasionally being passed by a Model T Ford on the cobblestone roads, I was completely amazed. I had never seen such buildings, such huge windows, or cars in those kinds of numbers. It was another world.

We got out at one of the stops, and I followed my Amish dad through all of those regular people to one of the larger buildings in the city. We went inside and climbed into an elevator—now that was an experience! I didn't know what to think when we walked into the closet (the elevator) and stood there. What were we waiting for? Then it started on its way up, and I really didn't know what was going on. I only knew that it felt like the elevator was coming out from under me.

We only went up a few floors, but I was happy to leave the elevator behind me.

Sometimes when Dad went into the city on his own, he would treat himself to some raw oysters, but he didn't do that when I was along. But there was this one trip where Dad bought me a lollipop, and it cost one penny. That was a big deal to me, that my dad would do that.

I guess this is where I tell you more about my dad, but to be honest, I don't know that much about him besides the basic facts. It wasn't like he ever sat down with us and told us stories about his youth, his parents, or what it was like growing up at the beginning of the 20th century. He was born in 1896, and he died in 1988. His mother had been ninety-eight years old when she passed, and she had a sister who lived to be 103 and another sister who made it to 107.

The sister who lived to 107 died in 1944, and I remember going to the funeral. I would have been thirteen years old or so. Joe told me later in life that she was alive when Jesse James was roaming the Wild West, and she even viewed Abraham Lincoln when his casket was put into a caboose and pulled from Philadelphia to Pittsburgh at the speed of five miles per hour. People lined up all along the railroad tracks to get a sight of him, and she was a teenager, part of that piece of history.

But my dad never talked about his own childhood. For a

long time, I wondered about it. I wondered what kind of childhood you could have that would make you so quiet, never talking to your own children. I wondered what his relationship was like with his own father.

I guess some things you'll never know.

Chapter Seven
The First Television

World War II started when I was around eight years old and went until I was nearly fourteen, and while I remember hearing about it occasionally in the news, I wasn't old enough, and didn't have enough schooling, to follow it or read about it. What would I have thought, as a young teenager, if someone had told me that in less than ten quick years, I'd be serving in the United States military, fighting a war in Korea? I didn't even know where Korea was when I was a kid. What a strange thought that would have been to me.

Our parents, being Amish, had no concern with educating us on the outside world—not what was going on or what people thought about what was going on. The Amish people in general kept the outside public life away from their children as much as they could. I guess there is always a fear among the Amish that if they learned too much about the wide world, they'd leave the Amish when the time came. I guess that didn't hold true for us, though—nearly all of us left the Amish, even though we grew up with almost no knowledge of the outside world.

Our life was a bubble—family, church, work. But my parents could never keep everything out, and every so often I'd see something that would give me such a hunger for what was going on outside of my own small community.

Like when I saw my first television. Of course, I don't mean our television—we didn't have a television in our house. Amish kids might have tried to hide a radio, but a TV? That was definitely off limits. I was around twelve when I started hearing about these things called *televisions* showing up in the non-Amish community around us. The first one I ever saw was a tiny thing, about a foot square, with a black-and-white picture. I was invited to go along with my brothers to the Fishers Hotel in Kinzers to watch a championship boxing match, and let me tell you, I was fascinated by that incredible television.

Later, we didn't really have televisions in Korea during the war. When Jean and I got married, her parents had a little black-and-white TV, and every night when I got home from work, the two of us would watch *The Lone Ranger* or other stories that we enjoyed together.

But that was far in the future, and if anyone had told me that's what my own future held, that I'd have a television someday, well, it would have been hard to believe.

Chapter Eight
Hired Out Again

When I was thirteen, I was hired out again, this time to a farm in Mount Pleasant, which was about a seven- or eight-mile walk. I walked there every Monday morning and walked home every Saturday night. I don't know why I was allowed to come home on Sundays—maybe my parents realized how distressed I had been during the previous times they had hired me out. I don't remember this particular hiring out being as hard on me as the first one. Maybe it was because I was older, or maybe it was because the owner was a nice guy to work for.

This farm was owned by Ike Kauffman, and he was married to my dad's youngest sister. He had some cattle, and my main job was taking care of them while he took care of the chickens. Ike was a lot younger than my own parents, so he had a different outlook on life, was a little more laid back than the old-timers. But I still got homesick there, and I often cried myself to sleep. Even at thirteen, I didn't like being away from home.

During the time I worked for Ike, I found an old bicycle, fixed it up, and started riding it to his house and back. It was practically downhill all the way home from that farm, so I coasted most of the way, but since we were Amish, I wasn't technically allowed to have a bike, so as soon as I got within sight of the house, I'd hide the bike in the woods. Those were always heart-pounding moments, when I'd steered into the trees and lay the bike down, covered it with leaves and branches, hoping the whole time that Dad didn't see me. If he would have caught a glimpse of that bike, he would have gotten rid of it, and I never would have seen it again—I can tell you that for sure.

Then, on Monday morning, when it was time to go back to Ike's farm, I'd pulled my bike from the woods and meet the milkman, who my family knew. He would put the bike on his truck for me, and I'd ride along with him, all the way to the farm in Mount Pleasant. He was also the milkman for Ike's farm, so it worked out perfectly.

As my own children and grandchildren grew up, and especially when they got to the ages of eleven, twelve, and thirteen (the same age I was when I was hired out to work on other farms), I would look at them and wonder, *Did I really have to do all that work when I was so young? I'd never ask them to do that.* It was almost unbelievable to me, that my parents had sent me out at such an age.

But that was just the way of life back then—we all had to do what we could to help the family and make sure we were all going to eat, all going to survive. When you grow up that way, you don't know any different. It was hard, of course, but we all had to work that way back then, so it didn't seem unfair. That's just how it was.

That's not to say it didn't affect me. There was the homesickness, but I think because I never really shared what I was thinking or feeling, it made me angry, and I had tantrums from time to time. I did things in my anger that I could barely remember later on.

One time my siblings and I were in the house and they did something that made me mad, and I went outside, up to the cellar door steps, and pounded on the window. I was so mad I could barely think straight. And as I was pounding on the window, the glass broke. I stared at it, confused as to what had happened. How had I done that?

My dad gave me a whipping for that.

Sometimes, when I was a kid, I just felt so helpless, and I guess that came out of me in these temper tantrums. I can't say I understand it or that it was right. It just was.

Chapter Nine
The Old Victrola

For most of my childhood, us kids didn't have much liberty to do what we wanted. But quite a few of us had musical minds, and what I mean by that is we really loved music. I think the majority of us kids were like that. So, when I was about fourteen, a few of us put our money together and bought an old Victrola record player that played 78s. You could carry it around in a little satchel. It was one with a big disk and you'd have to crank it to make it play, and you'd have to keep cranking it if you wanted it to play at full speed.

Oh, what joy that old thing brought us! We listened to Roy Acuff sing country music and play his fiddle, and we listened while Little Jimmy Dickins played the banjo. He was the oldest of thirteen children, and I thought he must know what it was like to be in a big family like ours.

Of course, being Amish, and having strict parents, we weren't technically allowed to have a record player, so we hid it up in the pigeon pen in the barn and only listened to it on nights when Mom and Dad went away. Sometimes, when they went off to church meetings or to spend time with relatives who lived close, we would even invite some neighbor friends into the barn to listen with us. It was a really big deal, something we loved.

One weekend, Mom and Dad went away to an all-day church affair, so we got out the Victrola and enjoyed it all weekend. We put it away before our parents arrived home, and then a few weeks later, when they went away again, we went up to listen. But this time, when I went to the place where we usually hid it, it wasn't there.

We searched the entire farm, and we couldn't find it. That was a big disappointment. I had a feeling Dad had found it and gotten rid of it, but he never said anything, and we surely weren't going to ask him about it. So, we all went on pretending nothing had happened. This happens in Amish families a lot, about a lot of things—stuff happens, and people just don't say anything.

The following spring, I was working with my dad out in the meadow. One of our major spring projects every year was fence-mending. We'd make our way around all the fences, make sure everything was strong and standing, and replace posts if necessary. I was digging a new posthole when my shovel clanged on something strange, something that didn't feel quite like a rock or anything else I'd ever dug into. I kept going, a little more carefully, and soon I realized it was the Victrola.

"Vas is das?" I asked my dad, pulling it out of the hole.

33

"What is this?" He just looked at me for a moment, then turned around and didn't say anything. I was so mad that he would take something from us kids, something that we loved so much.

When I went back to the house, I took it up to my mom and showed her what I'd found. I don't know if I was expecting her to be surprised or what, but she got a big kick out of it, thought it was hilarious. She just sat there laughing at the whole situation.

"I don't think it's very funny," I said, storming out. So many of us kids loved music and didn't have any outlet for that. I thought it was pretty lousy, actually, that my own dad would take something like a record player and bury it in the ground.

I don't remember having many friends outside of the family—my friends were always my brothers and sisters, or maybe cousins, but we just didn't get out enough to meet other people and make friends. And even if we would have had time to spend away from home, we didn't have any money to do anything.

Most of our life was spent working hard, but we were kids, so we still managed to sneak in some good fun every once in a while. Unfortunately, we didn't have much around the farm to have fun with, so we had to get creative.

We had a place down at the Pequea Creek, a swimming hole where we gathered on the weekends. And when we played baseball, we used a walnut as the ball, and we had this big wide board for a bat. For the bases, we used dried up piles of cow manure. There were five or six of us around the same age, old enough to play baseball with a walnut, and a few of the neighbors would come over and join us, so we had a good time playing ball.

We didn't have much, but we made do with what we had, and we had some good times, that's for sure. Even though they were hard times, there were good times. We did our chores in the morning and the evening, but during the day, if we had time, we'd go out and have a little fun.

Another fun thing we did was build our own go-cart. We had a running gear with four wheels, and we put a plank on the springs, arranging it so that it reached from the front to the back. After that, all we needed was an engine, so we enticed a cow or a heifer with a bucket of feed, grabbed on to their tails, and those animals would pull us through the field. Benny and Eli were always in the middle of anything like that.

The toys we had, we made ourselves. The fun we had, we figured out on our own. It was a hard childhood, sure, but I think in every childhood, kids will figure out how to have fun.

When Christmas came around, it wasn't a tree covered in lights with mounds of presents waiting beneath it. No, Christmas was a simple affair—we would each get an orange, some peanuts, and one gift that we could all share. One year, we got a wagon, and let me tell you, that was a huge deal. And our birthdays? Those were just ordinary days, nothing special.

When my kids threw a birthday party to celebrate my 80th birthday, that was the first birthday party I had ever had just for myself. Can you believe that? The kids surprised me, and then when they found out it was my first one, they had a party for me just about every year after that.

Chapter Ten
Telling Mom

The thing is, the Amish church doesn't give you much information on the Bible. Not any, really. The Bible they use is German, which is hard, if not impossible, to understand, even if you speak Pennsylvania Dutch. There was no Sunday School within the Amish church to help explain religious or theological concepts to kids as they got older. There just isn't a very deep knowledge of the Bible within the Amish community, certainly not like there is in most Christian communities.

It seemed like if you asked any questions about the Bible, no one wanted to answer . . . and they weren't very happy that you asked any questions in the first place. They never could give me good answers. I stopped asking questions when I was young because I could tell my questions weren't welcome.

The bishops and the preachers weren't much better when it came to biblical knowledge, at least not the ones that I knew. I was really curious when I was a boy, and I wanted to be saved. I wanted to know about God. But the Amish religion is more of a cultural thing—not so much a religious thing.

For example, one of the bishop's main roles was to monitor how you were dressed, to check on how you combed and cut your hair—that's the kind of thing they really paid attention to. I'll never forget the time my brother Eli and I were part of a threshing rig down at Ephraim King's house, and what my brother said to that bishop.

The threshing rigs were what people used to harvest their wheat, to separate the wheat from the grain. When you were on the threshing crew, you followed the threshing rig around the area. There were four people on the crew: the guy who fed the wheat into the rig; one in the bailer stringing the wires for the bails; the third guy carried the wheat from where it came out of the spout back into the granary; and the fourth, who ran the rig.

It was hard, hard work, and I was around fourteen years old, working like a man. I didn't know any different. Dad got all of my money, which I expected, since our family had so many needs.

Anyway, we went into the house for dinner and Ephraim King had a cigar in his mouth and asked all the men if they would like a cigar from his box. He offered it around. My brother Eli had already joined the church, and smoking cigarettes was definitely not allowed, but you could smoke cigars. This bothered my brother to no end.

So, when Ephraim got to him and asked if he wanted a

cigar, he shook his head no. "I don't want a cigar, but I sure could go for a cigarette." And he pulled one out and lit it. He just sat there smoking his cigarette like there was nothing wrong with it, but the older men smoking their cigars were uncomfortable.

Ephraim, our bishop, didn't say anything there on the spot, but a few days later, he and one of the preachers in our church came to our house bright and early. In fact, when we walked out to do our morning chores at 4:30 a.m., the two men were standing there.

"You'll need to come to church on Sunday and ask forgiveness for what you did," one of the men said.

"What did I do?" Eli asked.

"You smoked a cigarette," the man replied

So, the next Sunday, Eli went to church. I wasn't there but Joe told us all about it afterward. I guess they put Eli up at the front of the church and said what he had done was wrong.

"Why did you smoke a cigarette?" they asked him in front of the entire church. I guess that was his cue to take the humble road of repentance. He wasn't quite ready for that.

"Why do you smoke cigars?" he said to Ephraim, the bishop.

"Behave yourself," my father hissed.

After that, Eli didn't say anything more. But he left the Amish church soon after that, and that incident stuck with me. It was just another example in my young life of things not making sense in my own community, and it reinforced the desire I'd had for a long time to leave, to strike out and do something on my own.

It was when I was fourteen or fifteen that I had a kind of revelation. My family still went to the Amish church at that time, and I suddenly resolved, I can't remember why, but I resolved that I was going to go to church that day and really listen. I was going to pay attention as best as I possibly could, just to see what I could get out of it. I guess I figured I hadn't been paying much attention at church for most of my life, and that maybe, if I really give it a shot, I'll pick up on something important, something that will help me or point me in the right direction. Maybe it would all make sense. I think I was looking for a reason to stay Amish, and I wondered if listening to God would help me figure that out.

Well, we got to church that Sunday, and I was all ears. I tried really hard to pay attention. I was eager to listen, hoping that would make a difference in my life. But the problem was, the preachers spoke in High German, which I couldn't understand. I tried, though. We sat there as a family (men on one side of the room, women and children on the other side), and I listened for two hours, then there was a little recess, and then two more hours passed.

And as more and more time went by, I became more and more frustrated, because even though I had finally shown up ready to learn, ready to take in what I could, I couldn't understand a thing they were saying! I could understand a word here and there, but for the most part, I was lost.

That day, I walked out of Amish church and never went back. Never. I just told my parents the next church Sunday that I was finished. Of course, neither of them were okay with it, but by then I didn't care anymore. I couldn't do it. I was done.

Later that same summer, all of us kids were sitting in a circle outside helping with the canning. I can't remember which fruit or vegetable we were working with that particular day—depending on the time of year, we'd can peaches or shell peas or husk corn, all of us in a circle, everyone helping. Those are some of the good memories from my childhood, me and my brothers and sisters, gathered together, and even though we were working, we'd try to make it fun.

I remember on that one particular afternoon, probably getting close to dusk, all the other kids had left the circle and gone back into the house. Mom just kept working quietly, and I stood up and crossed the circle and sat down beside her. For a while we kept working together, just the two of us. It is one of the few moments in my entire life that I remember being with my mom, just the two of us.

"Mom," I said quietly. "You know, I don't want to be an Amish boy. I want to go out on my own."

She kept working, not saying anything at first. I thought surely she'd heard me, but she wasn't responding, so I felt I had to say it again.

"Mom, I don't want to be Amish when I'm older. I just can't do it."

That's when I realized she was crying, and that made me cry. So we sat there in the gathering dark, both of us crying. I was sad, but it felt good, too, getting that off my chest and finally telling her. I knew I'd be okay.

In those days, Mom was the one to come to our rooms in the morning and wake us up, call us to go do the chores, usually around 4:30 a.m. And I didn't want to frighten her, so I gave her a heads up.

"Some morning," I said to my mother, "you're going to come up to wake us, and I'm not going to be there. I just don't want you to be worried about me, because I'll be okay."

She cried and I cried. But that's how things happened, about a year and a half later, when I finally worked up the nerve to leave.

Chapter Eleven
Joe's Accident

When my older brother Joe was in rumspringa, sixteen or seventeen years old and running around, something happened that affected him for the rest of his life.

There were these teenagers down in Paradise who would run up to passing buggies and try to snatch the hats off of the Amish youth as they drove past. I'm not sure why they did it—I guess they thought it was fun and daring, or maybe they just wanted to cause trouble. I suppose I'll never know.

Anyway, Joe and Katie, my brother and sister, were driving their open-top buggy back from a hoedown or some party they had been to. It was before my time of running around, so I hadn't been there. These three guys started following them and kept trying to grab Joe's hat, but they couldn't get it. I guess they got frustrated and one of them threw a rock, hit Joe right in the temple. And it knocked him out cold.

When the buggy arrived home, Katie came running into the house and told us what happened. It was around midnight, so the rest of us were in bed, but the commotion woke us all up. I went down into the room where they laid Joe until a neighbor came and took Mom and Joe to the hospital. It was such a tragedy.

Turns out, being struck by the rock gave him serious brain damage, and it took him about a year before he got over most of the side effects. Even after that, he had a little bit of a slur in his speech for the rest of his life. It was hard on all of us, seeing him like that for so long, lying in bed, unable to work. I think for my mom, it was another sad thing in a long line of sad things, and it took her down low again.

Not too long after it happened, someone found out who did it. The police came and picked up Dad, and they drove him over to the house of the teen who threw the rock, and my dad forgave him. Nothing more ever came of it.

I guess forgiving those teenage boys was what the Amish were known for. They still are known for forgiveness. For my dad, doing that seemed like the right thing to do. It didn't seem right to me, though, even when I was so young. I thought those boys had hurt Joe bad, and I didn't see why they should get off so easy. But Dad remained very low-key through the entire incident.

I have to admit, though, as I got older, I had this nagging question in the back of my mind.

Why could Dad forgive that stranger for injuring Joe so seriously, but he couldn't forgive me for leaving the Amish?

Chapter Twelve
Out on My Own

The thing is, almost all of us kids were ambitious—we all had a lot of entrepreneurial spirit. We were rambunctious and motivated. When I was thirteen, fourteen, fifteen years old, I really believed that I could be whatever I wanted to be, and I had a great desire to be something. I wanted to be independent and have a good family. I wanted to get out of that small world I lived in and do something big.

Then I turned sixteen in June of 1947. The Second World War was only a few years behind us, and the country was trying to recover from a bad couple of decades. World War I, The Spanish Flu, The Great Depression, World War II, and the atomic bomb . . . No one really knew what was going to happen next, and the world seemed an unstable place to be.

But I knew one thing—I was leaving the Amish.

Once I was sixteen, I could start rumspringa, sewing my wild oats, and I started going with the other youth in the area to hoedowns and other gatherings. I lasted until January, and then I got serious about leaving. I knew it was time to start the rest of my life. I heard about a dairy farmer who was looking for someone to run his dairy, so I walked over for an interview.

"Do you think you can handle this whole dairy?" the farmer asked, looking at me a little skeptically. After all, I was just a sixteen-year-old kid, getting ready to head out on my own.

I looked at him without a single doubt. "I know I can handle this dairy." That was all I said.

He hired me for twenty-five dollars a week. Pretty good money for a teenager in those days.

That same weekend, I went out and got my hair cut, something which was a last straw of sorts. There was no turning back after I got my hair cut short. That was completely against the Amish tradition. The next morning, after chores, I showed up in the kitchen along with all of my brothers, like we did every week. And Dad came in and made sure we had all brushed our hair and then checked it for length, to make sure we were all still within the Amish rules, like he did every week. Well, he saw my hair and didn't say much, but I could tell he was angry. I think he sensed I was on the edge of leaving, that I'd soon be gone.

He leaned in. "If you leave," he said quietly, "don't you ever come back here for help if you need it."

That was a little surprising, and when he said it, it kind of caught me off guard. I hadn't expected him to say something like that, but I just stood there and took it. And I vowed to myself I'd never go home for help, no matter what. Never. I'd make it on my own. Even if I was starving.

On Sunday night, I wrapped everything that was important to me in a handkerchief and walked out of the house. To be honest, that handkerchief was pretty empty. I think I took a shaving kit, but I didn't have much besides that because I was still young and hadn't bought many things for myself. The stars were bright that night, and it was cold. And I went down to work at John Landis's farm to run his dairy.

There was a guy in town on Queen Street, Easy Credit Milt, and he had all kinds of clothes you could buy, even on credit. All the Amish boys knew about this place and when they wanted to buy some English clothes, that's where they went. But I didn't have any money when I left home, so I went there and bought a pair of jeans, a shirt, and some shoes, and I paid him back over the next couple of months.

The next problem I had was how to get around. I definitely didn't have enough money for a car. The neighbor across the street heard about me leaving the Amish, and he had a body shop. He gave me a 1937 Ford Coupe for fifty dollars. When I told him I didn't have fifty dollars, he smiled. "Just take it and pay me when you can." That thing was a little 4-cylinder, and when I got to a hill, I had to change gears or I'd never make it up the hill, but it was a godsend.

I didn't return home for a visit until Mother's Day, four months later, and I certainly had thoughts spinning through my mind as I came up the lane, wondering how it would go. I didn't know for sure how it would be—I had heard of other kids who came home after they left the Amish and their parents just told them to turn back around and leave.

It was a nice spring day. I just walked in and said, "Hi, Mom." We didn't hug or anything—hugging didn't happen in our house. We never told each other, "I love you." That just wasn't how we interacted.

But it was a nice visit, maybe a little strange being home and not being Amish anymore. My mom and I spent some time catching up, but Dad wasn't in the house when I was there. He didn't come inside once. Maybe that's because it wasn't a big deal—there were so many of us siblings, and others had already left the Amish, so there wasn't much fuss. Or maybe he didn't come in because he didn't want to see me. I guess I'll never know.

I was happy with how it went.

Around that time, my sister Anna Ruth was thinking she wanted to leave, too. She ended up going to nursing school, and I really encouraged her through that and helped her with some of the costs, whenever I could. Later, she would marry Steve Petersheim, and he would become a good friend of mine. Anna Ruth and I always had a close connection.

I kept working for John Landis, running his dairy, until I turned eighteen. I lived there on the farm with them, and John was an aggressive sort of business man—he not only had a dairy, but he also raised broilers, chickens that he kept for twelve weeks before selling on to chicken processors. That was the main reason he brought me in to look after the dairy, so that he could focus on the chickens. The farm was set up so that he raised the crops needed to feed the chickens and the dairy cows: corn, some oats, but no tobacco. He was a smart farmer, and I learned a lot there, watching how he ran it like a business.

I worked there for two years, until 1949 when I turned eighteen. John pretty much left the dairy operation up to me. I was used to working with dairy cows, so I had no problems. And as I lived there, I realized they were really nice people, he and his wife. They went to the Mennonite church. They were a young couple when I first arrived—soon after, his wife had her first baby, and soon after I left, they had their second child.

"I guess I'm ready to leave the farm and go find some work out in the world," I told him soon after I turned eighteen.

"Oh, don't do that!" he said. "If you go out and do public work, you'll end up in the service. You'll have to serve in the Korean War."

I shrugged. "If I have to go into the service, so be it. But I'm going out into the public to work."

That was in June of 1949, and I finished out the summer there at the farm before I decided to hitchhike to Florida. I had relatives in Pinecraft, and I thought I'd try to get a job there. I needed a change of scenery, and I wanted to do something interesting.

Well, that was my intention, anyway, but as soon as I told one of my friends, Jake Kauffman, what I planned on doing, he said he wanted to go, too. And he had a car, which was handy, so he drove us both down. Back in those days, there was no Route 95 to follow—it was 301 all the way down, and it took around thirty-six hours of driving to get there.

When Jake and I got down there, I met up with some friends who were staying at this motel called Carvell Court; definitely nothing fancy, but they said I could stay with them.

It took me a day or two to find a job—not too long. I was

hired by the Manatee River Hotel in Bradenton, Florida, to work in room service as a bus boy. It was like nothing I'd ever done before. I was just a naïve little Amish boy serving aristocrats, the upper crust, and members of the Pittsburgh Pirates baseball team who stayed there during spring training. I didn't know what a filet was or what anyone meant by wanting their steak cooked "rare." Fortunately, all I had to do was serve it.

I spent a lot of time with the ball players, even becoming friendly with some of them, but to be honest, I didn't understand them that much, or what they did for a living, because my family had never really been into sports.

That was a strange job for me to have, and I had to feel my way through it. But they gave me a room, and I took my meals there in the hotel, so it felt like I was set. My salary was almost nothing, but I did get tips.

I decided to go back home in March of the following spring and worked for a silo crew, building silos. I enjoyed the work, and the heights we worked at didn't bother me in the least, something I didn't think about much at the time, but later in my life would serve me well. Those were long days, but the money was decent. And life went on.

The whole time, there was a war waging on the other side of the world, but we didn't hear much about it. What would a war thousands of miles away have to do with me or the people I loved? What did I care about communism or the border between North and South Korea? I didn't know a single thing about it.

Not until I got drafted.

Chapter Thirteen
Off to the Korean War

It happened in October of 1952, soon after I had turned nineteen. I received a registered letter from the United States government stating that I had been drafted and needed to report to the draft board in Lancaster, PA. This didn't surprise me—I knew that my age group had started getting called in. In fact, some of my friends had already been drafted; a few of them were even in Korea by then.

And it wasn't that going to war or serving my country scared me. I wasn't afraid to join the armed forces. I guess I just had that typical nineteen-year-old mind-set, that, in the end, nothing bad would happen to me. That I would do what needed to be done. That I'd survive.

I got a physical around that time, which I easily passed,

and was given a few weeks to report. I made my way around to my friends, but it didn't seem like a huge deal at the time.

I had no idea what I was getting into.

I went by the house to say good-bye to my mom before I left for basic training. I was the third one in my family to leave for the service, so it wasn't easy for her. She had already been forced to say good-bye to two of her sons, Benny and Eli. I was told she used to sit back in her bedroom, rarely coming out, and pray that each of us boys would come home safe and sound. Sometimes she wouldn't leave her room for days at a time. And she waited, all while my older brother Benny spent a year in Korea, and my brother Eli spent time in Austria. I guess that's how it goes.

I never did see my dad or get a chance to say good-bye to him before I left, and that didn't bother me.

I reported for duty at Fort Belvoir in Fairfax, Virginia in the fall of 1952 for basic training. I arrived in pretty good shape from building silos—I didn't have an ounce of fat on me, and I passed all my physicals and sailed through basic with flying colors. I took to the rigid lifestyle pretty well. I had gotten used to following orders from my dad my whole life; and I was used to waking up early and working hard all day; and the Amish community kind of trained you to get used to doing what the people above you told you to do, so the army didn't seem like that much of a transition.

Right after basic training, they shipped us out.

As I said, I wasn't afraid when I got my call to go into the service. Maybe I didn't really know what was going on over there, or maybe it was just because I was like every other teenage boy who couldn't possibly imagine he'd ever die. When I left for the

Far East, I wasn't afraid.

Another reason I wasn't afraid is because I was surrounded by 140 other soldiers. When you're with a group like that, and you look around, you figure the group can handle whatever comes your way. By then, we knew why we were going, or at least the basics of it, and the army oriented us pretty well in regard to what we should expect when we got there. We were mostly just ready to get going. You can only sit around preparing to go to war for so long.

The first thing we did was head to Seattle, Washington, and from there, we boarded a troop ship and sailed to Japan. I felt like such a tiny cog in the whole machine, a little Amish boy seeing Seattle? Sailing the Pacific? Arriving in Japan? It was like the whole world opened up. I had only ever known Lancaster—the edge of my world was Strasburg or Lancaster city, or, a little later, Bradenton, Florida. But there I was, crossing the Pacific. It was quite a thing.

It was my first time ever at sea, in that huge boat, and there were four thousand of us altogether, from all over the country. We sailed from Seattle to Japan, and fortunately, I didn't get motion sickness—but a lot of the guys got really sick. In fact, on the way over, we ran into a small typhoon, rode up and over thirty-foot waves, and that boat shuddered in the storm. But it didn't bother me at all. There were other guys who threw up the entire trip.

But eventually the storm calmed and we arrived in the Far East. What an experience.

In Japan, we got on an old steam-engine train and rode it clickety-clack all the way south, and that was where we prepared to enter Korea. The sergeant stood in front of all of us kids, we were all sitting on the ground, and warned us of what was about to happen.

"I want to tell you kids something," he said in a booming voice. "We're gonna make a beach landing. All you guys are going to have your gear on, and if you can't swim with sixty pounds on your back, you're done."

Can you imagine that? I could hear everyone around me fretting and muttering about that beach landing. Some of us could swim, but even if you were a marginal swimmer, who could possibly swim with sixty pounds pulling them under? I'll tell you, we were worried about that. That was the first time in the whole ordeal when I began to have some reservations or felt any fear.

A day or so later, in the early morning, we boarded a troop ship that took us to Incheon, Korea. We were divided into groups of seven and put into PT boats, so that when the mouth of the big boat opened, these little PT boats spilled out and headed for shore. I tell you, I was nervous. How was I going to swim with sixty pounds on my back? And what if the enemy was firing at us when we landed? We just had no idea what to expect.

You boarded these little boats in alphabetical order, and since I was an *F*, I was in pretty early. The boat slammed into the water, and we were buzzing toward shore. We got within about one hundred yards, and the mouth of the boat opened up, and our squad leader was shouting at us to crawl on out, so we did. I got into the water and thought, *Oh, man, here we go. This is it.*

Imagine my surprise, all of our surprise, when we realized the water wasn't any deeper than our waists. And I'm not that tall. Imagine our relief when we could wade onto shore and not a shot was fired, and no one got pulled under the water by their packs! We set up camp there and stayed for a couple of months.

During one spell of my time in Korea, it was so cold that we were each given sleeping bags, and we were living in a pit in the woods. We were on constant blackout so as not to give away our position—we weren't allowed to so much as light a match. Preparing for breakfast the next morning meant keeping a can of sea rations between our legs at night while we slept, so that it the morning it would be thawed out enough to dig from the can. That was breakfast. Those were tough times, but we had been taught to survive in basic training, and that was that. There wasn't any point complaining—you got what you got, and the days passed that way.

Eventually, we built a compound fence around our battalion and more or less settled in that area. At first, we had no running water—we either drank water that was trucked in, or we boiled water from the area. But someone got the idea to build a water silo, and I let it be known that I had worked on silos back home, so they involved me in the project. I even took the lead, as the whole thing continued. We finished building that silo, and it was a success.

"Fisher," the company commander said to me one day. "I understand you did a good job building that silo."

"Yes, sir. Thank you, sir."

"We need four more."

He paused. I was kind of surprised he was telling me about it. I figured there were other, more senior people he would talk to about such things.

"Will you take on the responsibility to do the work?"

"Yes, sir," I said. But I paused. "Sir?"

"Yes, Fisher?"

"I'll need some help."

"I'll give you four guys," he said.

"Excuse me, sir, but how will these guys work for me?"

"Fisher?"

"Well, sir, we're all the same rank. I won't have any authority over them. Why would they listen to me?"

He thought about it for a second and nodded. "Fine. We'll make you a corporal."

So, I had these four guys working for me and the five of us built four more silos. It took us maybe six months. They were twelve feet in diameter and about forty feet tall, sitting on stilts with the silo on top. They fed water by gravity throughout the entire compound—the water was trucked in and then pumped into the silos, which we used for showering and cooking and anything else we needed water for.

This meant we could take showers on a more regular schedule. Those shower stalls were about thirty feet long and had twenty shower heads, all of them out in the open, no privacy whatsoever. It was kind of strange at first, but I got used to it. Seemed like after some time passed, the same group of guys took showers at the same time. Everyone had their own habits, I guess, and when you're living in close quarters like that, you get used to each other.

The bathrooms were nearby and were nothing more than a trough—you peed in the trough, and everything ran downhill into a tank.

Building those silos was actually quite a long project, and

by the time we finished, the company commander (or "Old Man" as we all referred to him), called me in to talk again.

"Fisher."

"Yes, sir."

"You did good work on those silos."

"Thank you, sir."

"I'd like to keep you here in the compound. You can be in charge of the welding shop, the carpentry shop, and oversee everything in that regard."

"Yes, sir."

I had a very good relationship with the first sergeant and the company commander, mostly because I was never afraid to do anything they asked me to do. So that's where I stayed for the rest of my time in the service, running those shops, and that was fine with me. No going out into the field. No getting called to battles or skirmishes. I was in charge of the shop until I was mustered out, fifteen months after I arrived. By the time I got home, I was coming up on twenty-one years old.

I'm glad I did it, but I wouldn't want to do it again. We got there toward the end of the war, and that time in the trench, for five or six weeks, wasn't pleasant at all. Sometimes we were asked to defend the trench. It was a dirty, cold, miserable place.

We were paid $120 per month for our service and an extra fifty dollars a month for time spent in the trench. I guess that was hazard pay. You could send as much money home every month as you wanted, so I sent everything home to a bank account except for ten dollars. We also received weekly rations that included a carton of cigarettes, a six-pack of beer, and toilet articles. We got those every Thursday. Well, I didn't smoke and I didn't care much for beer, so I sold my cigarettes and beer to the barber, and he'd sell them on to his buddies. Of course, I waited until Tuesday to sell them to him because by then, everyone who wanted beer and cigarettes had run out, and he could get a premium. I guess I was a business man even then.

I also had a good dog in the army—his name was Archie. He was the base's dog, but because of the work I did on the base, I had a room of my own, and he slept with me every night. When it came time for me to go back to the States, I really wanted to bring Archie with me, but they said I wasn't allowed.

By the time I got home from Korea, I had saved up several thousand dollars, and one of the first things I did was buy a brand new 1954 Mercury Marquis, a hard top, a real cat wagon.

But after I returned home, even though I tried to play it off, something in me had changed. I had lost two friends while we were up at the North Korean border, two guys I went through basic training with. We had been shipped over there together, in the same battalion. It was strange to think that they never came home, that I'd made it back to my home and my friends and my family, but they never did. That weighed on me.

Those were the only two casualties who I knew personally. One of them was from Pittsburgh—his name was George Slaughter. The other guy's name was Carson, but I can't remember his last name. I guess that was a long time ago. Their deaths bothered me for quite some time after I got back, and because the public wasn't happy with the nation's involvement in Korea, it wasn't something I talked about.

Some of the Korean War Veterans went through hell over there, and yet there was this general sense that people didn't appreciate what we had done. When we got back, none of us wanted to tell people we were veterans of the Korean War, because you didn't know how people would respond.

So, I just never talked about it.

Never.

If someone didn't know me personally, they never would have known I served—most Korean vets never flaunted their service. We weren't recognized hardly at all until the 2010s, but now we're few and far between. I was one of the younger ones to serve in that war, and I'm eighty-nine now. The older ones would be in their mid-nineties. There aren't many of us left, not anymore.

Chapter Fourteen
Jean

When I got back from the war, I was kind of in dire straits. I hitchhiked back to my parents' house and walked into the place, thinking I could live there for a bit until I got my feet back under me. I had just returned from war after all from the other side of the world. But I soon realized they didn't have room for me.

I didn't have a home.

Holy mackerel, I thought. *Here I am gone for almost two years fighting in a war, and now I don't have a place to sleep.* That was a sharp blow. It's not really something you expect after getting back from living in a trench and firing weapons and building things thousands of miles away. I was pretty depressed about it. I had a purpose over there, and people depended on me, and now I was back in Lancaster and didn't even have a bed to sleep in.

But as soon as my sister Suzie found out about it, she said, "Gid and I will give you a home. We'd be happy to have you." So I moved in with them and stayed there until I got married. What a relief! I loved the two of them, and it meant the world to me that they took me in when they did.

As I said earlier, before the war I worked for a guy building silos, and when I got back from Korea, the same guy offered me my job back, so that's what I did. But it was a lot of travel—we were building silos in five different states, and some weeks we'd be gone from Monday morning until Saturday night.

Then, in March of '55, I saw Jean for the first time.

Back when we were young people, one of the things we used to do was "drive the loop." The loop was basically a lap around the center of Lancaster city, starting at the center square where Queen Street crosses King. We drove north on Queen to Orange, then left on Orange, down to Prince where we turned left again, and then left on King and back to where we started. This was the thing to do and a way to meet people and hang out.

Lancaster was really hopping on those nights—there were vendors on the sidewalks selling peanuts and popcorn and shoe shine boys shouting out to the crowd, and the guys driving the loop were hollering at friends they saw on the sidewalks. You could get a hot dog for a dime and get your shoes shined for a quarter, which I seldom did because that was a lot of money back in the day. The nickel candy bars, though, they were in my price range.

The other thing about teenagers back then was that everyone smoked. It was the fad. If someone came into your house, the first thing they normally did was light a cigarette. That's just how it was. I can remember when the first cigarette machine came out—you'd put two dimes in, pull the lever, and a pack of Lucky Strikes fell from the machine along with three cents change, because cigarettes were 17 cents a pack. But the change didn't come out separately—it was three pennies encased in the plastic around the pack. That's how the cigarette packs were manufactured, because they planned on people paying 20 cents for a 17-cent pack.

One night I met up with an old buddy, Bob Stoltzfus. His dad was an ex-Amish guy, and his mom was very kind. They had a really special family. I ended up going to their place almost every Sunday, and Bob and I became best friends. That Stoltzfus family, they were a few of the people I really enjoyed when I got back from Korea.

Anyway, Bob came back from the war in December, two months after me, and we each purchased a car, and we both also started driving the loop together. That's where I met Jean for the first time—she was hanging out with a few of her cousins. Bob and I were pretty taken by these girls, and over the course of our conversation with them, we discovered that they liked to go roller skating at Rocky Springs.

Well, he and I happened to show up at Rocky Springs one night, and Jean and her cousins were there roller skating. That's when we had our first real conversation, and I realized that she was quite a gal, with a personality second to none, very vivacious and ambitious. You know, she was so much fun, and getting to know her is when I started to find out what life was really like, or what it could be like.

Jean showed me what love and affection were all about. I

had never really experienced that kind of simple affection before—I hadn't even seen it, not between my mom and dad or anyone, really. But Jean was so affectionate and loving and tender with me. It was quite a thing.

She came from a tough family. A good family, and a kind family, but her dad was a little rough around the edges, you might say. When we first started dating, we went down to her house, and she didn't want me to go inside. I couldn't figure out why, but I guess she was a little concerned that her dad might scare me off.

I finally went in and met her parents, Walter and Arlene Erb, down in Holtwood. Her mom was a special lady, and her dad was a bit crude, but I liked him a lot because he was a comical guy. And even though he only had a fourth-grade education, he could figure out just about anything. As someone who enjoyed working my hands, I could appreciate that about him.

Jean's family was in our life a lot, and that was a good thing. We spent a fair amount of time with her parents, and it seemed like Jean's extended family was getting together all the time.

Jean's parents were opposites. Walter was, to be quite honest, an alcoholic, and Arlene was so godly, she wouldn't touch a drop to drink and had her Bible in hand all the time. They were on very different pages as far as that was concerned. And she was rather timid while he was the life of the party, one of the funniest people I've ever known.

Walter had more common sense when it came to fixing things than I've ever seen. During prohibition, he had a distillery set up on a farm down in the holler. A group would come in and they'd run this thing for thirty days or so. I was dating Jean, and one evening Walter came up to me.

"Steve," he said, "let's take a little walk."

"Okay."

We walked down through the farm and he held up a flashlight and sent a code with it. Someone in the distance replied with their own flashlight signals. Then we walked down and he showed me his setup. Moonshine poured out of a pencil-sized tube.

"You have to try this, Steve."

"Sure," I said, so he put a little in a glass, and I took a sip. I nearly choked. It was 140-proof.

They would make several gallons at a time and then move out and sell it. It was quite a different scene than this little Amish boy had grown up in.

One time, Walter's dog got hit out on the road and got its leg broke. I came into the house that day and asked, "Where's Pap?"

"He's down in the basement, working on his dog."

What in the world? So, I went downstairs and there he was, bent over his dog, making a splint and fixing up his dog. Back then, if a dog broke a leg or something like that, most people probably would have put it out of its misery. But he put together a perfect splint, and the dog healed up nicely.

Another time, I got to Jean's house and, again, I asked, "Where's Pap?"

Well, the washing machine had broken. He was down in the basement again, this time taking the whole machine apart. It turns out those old motors had brushes, and when the brushes bumped up against the armature, the machine wouldn't run anymore. So he needed brushes for his ancient washing machine, which weren't available anymore. He took a battery out of a flashlight, cut it up, took one of the pieces and put it in the armature, and it started running again. He was brilliant in his own way.

The long and the short of it for me was, I was in love with Jean. I found her family to be kind, encouraging and affectionate. I started to think it was time to ask Jean to marry me.

Chapter Fifteen
Starting with High Steel

Jean and I dated all that summer of '55, and that's when I decided I didn't want to build silos anymore. It was too much travel, and I didn't want to always be out of town. I wanted to be with Jean. I thought I'd look into becoming a tradesman of sorts, and after thinking about it a bit, I pursued plumbing and welding.

I interviewed for a plumbing job, and they told me I could have it if I wanted it, but before I committed to them, I also went to High Steel for a welding interview. I got that job, too, and I decided welding was more for me, so I went to work for High. They had a small shop on Water Street, in the city, and that's where I started. It didn't seem like a big decision at the time, whether to become a plumber or a welder, but I realize now that it made all the difference.

Not long after High Steel hired me—I was the twelfth or thirteenth man they had hired, so I was pretty low on the ranking—they decided to move out of the city, and I was involved in helping them make that move. High Steel is where I learned how to weld. It really set me up for the next ten years of my life.

Now, I was young and eager and wanted to learn as much as I could, so while I was in training, I kept at it as much as I could. In the morning, at around nine thirty, they had a coffee break; then lunch was at noon; and then another coffee break at three thirty. During those coffee breaks, I would go down to the scrap pile and work on welding different materials. I was so interested in it.

One thing I had developed during my years as a silo builder was an ability to work anywhere, including a hundred feet off the ground, so when High Steel realized this, they put me on their tall jobs. They had just started building schools and warehouses and things like that. They asked if I was interested in hanging steel, working up off the ground, and I said I certainly was. So I became a steel rigger, and I hung steel for them for a number of years. That's where I learned more and more about the trade, and I did really well with it, because I had no fear of heights.

I really enjoyed rigging steel. I could climb a fifty-foot-high column as fast as you could walk away from me. If you've ever seen the steel skeleton of a building going up, then you've seen the work of a steel rigger. It begins with a detailed architectural rendering, and each piece of steel has a number, and everything gets put in place one piece at a time.

Back in those days, a steel rigger never tied off. If you were scared of heights, you didn't belong there. A lot of times, I'd be up five, six, even seven stories in the air without being tied to anything. I even set buildings as high as ten stories. The pieces come swinging in by crane, and I'd be there straddling the beam, waiting for the crane to bring in the next one. My motto was, always know where your feet and hands were and where they were going. Always. The concentration level had to be sky-high—you couldn't be up there thinking about other things. Rigging steel demands total focus.

We never had anyone fall while I was working at High Steel, but we did have some close calls. One time I was up cutting the top off a stack. The thing was 150 feet high and they wanted to take fifty feet off the top. Well, I got lifted up there and cut a hole in the stack. Then I climbed inside the stack and welded a couple of angles for me to sit on, as a stabilizer. The crane had hold of the top of the stack, and once I cut around the stack, I motioned for the crane operator to go ahead and take it away, but the top ring was heavier than we expected. When the crane took off the top, the whole thing swung around and crashed into the stack where I was sitting. One of the angles I was sitting on flew out from under me. Fortunately, I didn't get hit or fall through the stack—100 feet down.

The guy who owned High Steel at the time was Sanford High—he had gotten into the welding business and really grew it. He was a Mennonite man and a good man to work for. He was the main reason I chose welding over plumbing. He was a guy who, during the Depression, had run his welding business out of a cow stable and then got a little shop. We got along very well, and he became one of my favorite people in my life. What a good man.

To me, he was a first-class guy, and he really liked me, too. If he had a strange job to do, he'd take me out to look at it and ask if I thought we could do it. I'd say, "Sure, we can do that," and he'd nod his head and take the job. We had a great rapport with each other.

I settled in there at High Steel and started to make my way. I was a hard worker, determined to learn all I could about welding, and willing to do any job. The war was behind me, I wasn't Amish anymore, and I had a good job and a steady girlfriend.

I felt like I was finally getting ahead in life.

Chapter Sixteen
Providing for My Family

In February of 1956, Jean and I got married. My parents didn't come to the wedding—in those days, Amish people rarely attended non-Amish weddings, although these days that sort of thing is a little more common. But my brothers and sisters came. It was a plain little wedding in a quaint white church, Bethesda United Methodist Church, down in Holtwood.

We got married on a Saturday, and that night for our honeymoon we drove out to Carlisle, a little town about fifty miles west of Lancaster. We spent the night there, then came back Sunday night and went straight to work on Monday morning. It didn't seem like a problem at the time. That's just how we did things. Money was something that I knew would come later—I was always confident in that—so it didn't bother me that we didn't get to go off for a week. Besides, I was excited to start my life with Jean. She had changed everything for me.

We lived with Jean's parents for most of the first year of our marriage, and let me tell you, we didn't have any money. Nothing. And in those days, I was always on the lookout for a way to make a little cash. I wanted something better for us than what I grew up with. I didn't want to always be scrambling around, trying to make ends meet. When I was a kid, I made the connection between us being poor and me being hired out to work for the summer, and that wasn't the kind of life I wanted for my family.

Jean got pregnant, and when she was about eight months along, I was really bothered because I just didn't know what we would do when this baby arrived. Jean was the executive secretary for one of the bosses down at the Holtwood power plant, and I didn't want Jean's mom to raise the baby. I wanted Jean to do that. In my opinion, a grandmother isn't supposed to raise her grandchildren, and a mother isn't supposed to be absent. I probably feel that way because of how it was with my own mother when I was growing up. One day when I got home from work, after supper, I asked Jean if she'd take a walk with me.

We wandered down through the woods.

"Jean," I said, "Look, I'd really like you to go down and tell your boss that you'll give him a couple of weeks' notice, and then you'll quit so that you can stay home and take care of our baby. From here on out, I'll take care of the rest."

I knew I could do it. I just knew it. I was determined to, anyway, and Jean believed me. It was a big financial sacrifice for us, her walking away from her job, but I was up for the challenge and felt strongly about it. The next day at work, she told her boss she would be quitting when the baby came, and she did.

As the years passed, this was such a weight off my mind. Even when I had long days or projects that stretched on, I knew Jean would always be there taking care of our kids, and I never had to worry about what was going on at home.

I don't think I ever saw her sit down, ever. She was always home when I got home from work, and the kids were at the dinner table, waiting for me. That was our family, and I loved them.

During that first year of our marriage, Jean's grandfather owned a farm close-by, and he said, "Steve, if you'd like to raise some tobacco here, you can have some land to do that."

It was very nice of him to do that, so I raised one acre of tobacco that year, and I sold it for three hundred and fifty dollars—quite a sum of money in those days.

An opportunity came along to buy a little house in Rawlinsville. We decided to go for it, and we bought it for $7,200 with a first and second mortgage. I was making sixty-five dollars per week in those days, which was pretty common as far as wages were concerned, but I also had this $350 from the sale of that tobacco, and that was the down payment.

The house was a cute little place just a few feet off the street that ran through the small town, if you can call Rawlinsville a town. It's really just an intersection of roads with a few dozen houses. The place had a nice front porch and a separate, two-bay garage out back. It felt like Jean and I were making our way.

That's really how we got started out in life. A few breaks here and there, an acre of tobacco, and a down payment on a house. That was the beginning.

Chapter Seventeen
Starting Out on My Own

So, there I was, married and working at High Steel making sixty-five dollars a week. Any opportunity I had to make a little extra money, I took it. My brother was in the silo business, so I helped him when I could. I worked overtime whenever extra hours were available at High Steel. And by 1962, I had my house paid off and no bills.

While I worked for High Steel, I had a chance to build a fire escape on the side for the guy who owned the gas station where I bought gas every week. This was interesting to me because it was a small job, and I could do it by myself or with just one other guy. I was happy for the opportunity and ended up getting a contract to build it. The contract was for $1,200, and I figured I needed about $300 for the steel.

I didn't realize it at the time, but this was the moment when everything would change. And a lot of the reason I was able to navigate into this new situation was because of how I had grown up. I may have had problems with my dad, but he had taught me how to work.

The problem was, the $300 I needed for the steel was more than a month's wages. If I was going to be able to do this job, I'd need to borrow the money up front for materials.

I went to Farmer's Bank and talked to the manager. I told him I had this contract to build a fire escape.

"How much do you need, Steve?" he asked me.

"About $300 to buy the steel," I explained. "I can pay you back when I finish the job, in three or four weeks."

This bank manager pulled out his drawer, opened a notebook, and signed a note for $300. I signed it, took it over to the cashier, and the cashier gave me $300.

"Go get the job done, Steve," the bank manager said with a smile.

That's how it was back then—if the bank trusted you, they would do wonders for you. We did our banking there for a long, long time. Now over sixty years later, I still remember their willingness to help me out in the early days.

Well, I went to work, built the fire escape, got paid for it, and a few weeks later I was back at the bank. I paid off the note, and the manager took it out of his desk and tore it up.

"Thanks, Stephen," he said.

After a few months of building more fire escapes, I went to Jean with my crazy idea.

"Jean," I said. "I don't like working for a paycheck. I feel like I could be doing more, making more."

"But Steve, you're doing pretty good."

"I know, but I don't like it. Would you care if I went into business for myself? I know what I want to do—I can make good money building fire escapes. Do you care if we put all we have on the line and start a business of our own?"

She hardly took any time to think about it. "Whatever you want to do, Steve. I trust you. I'll stand by you."

That was it.

I never would have accomplished what I did in my life without Jean, her trust and encouragement.

Sanford High was the man I needed to talk to. I was still working for him at the time, and I decided in November of that year that I wanted to go into business for myself. I knew if I didn't do it then, it would probably never happen. Besides, by that time I had seventeen fire escapes on order! I made up my mind that I'd tell Sanford about it the following Monday morning.

In those days, it didn't matter what time of day you went to his office—he was there. He loved that business and was determined to make it successful, keep it growing. I knocked on his door.

"Come in," he said, and when he saw it was me, he asked, "What are you doing here so early, Steve?"

"I need to talk."

"Okay, what's on your mind?"

"Sanford, I don't know what's going to become of this, but in February of next year, I want to leave here and go into business for myself."

He didn't say anything, so I kept going.

"I want to know, if things don't work out, if I don't make it, will I still have a job here? Would you hire me back?"

Sanford looked at me and without pausing even a second said, "I'll hire you back in a heartbeat."

I hadn't even sat down, and he came up out of his chair, walked around his desk, and gave me a hug.

"Good luck, Steve."

Sometimes, that's all we need. Someone to encourage us, believe in us, and send us off in the right direction. It always helped, too, especially in the early days, knowing I had that safety net of employment back at High Steel if I needed it. I hoped I wouldn't, I didn't think I would, but it took a weight off my mind knowing we wouldn't lose the house if I couldn't find enough work.

I started moving in the direction of working for myself. We operated out of our little two-car garage, and I purchased barely enough equipment to get by with: a big steel table, a welder and torch, and a few other tools. That was all I needed to start building railings and fire escapes.

One problem—I didn't have electricity in the garage. And I didn't have the money to pay an electrician, so I bartered with a neighbor, built the railing around his porch in exchange for him connecting electric to my garage.

I grew the business enough in a few short months, and I left High Steel in February. I took the leap, and I wasn't afraid of hard work. It paid off, because within six months, I was the key builder of fire escapes in Lancaster and the surrounding cities. I just seemed to get busier every week, getting new calls from people who heard I was doing that kind of work. And it was at this time that cities began requiring fire escapes for apartments on the third floor or higher.

Around this time, I heard about a guy I knew, an acquaintance, who had been laid off from an excavating company. I called and asked him if he could help me put up a fire escape. The installation was hard to do on my own, and there were a fair amount of times when I could have used an extra set of hands on site. He came and helped, and he ended up being an employee of mine for many, many years. Buddy Herr was his name. He joined us right in the beginning, when it was just me and Jean.

I turned out to have a lot of good work, and Jean helped me the whole time, painting steel in the shop and doing all kinds of odd jobs with me. She just did whatever it was that needed to get done. She was right there.

I started to have this vision that someday I could have a business where my kids could work, that if they wanted to work for me, they'd have that option. That was one of the main things that motivated me and gave me energy, this idea that what I was doing could turn into a family business, something that would stretch on beyond me and provide for my kids. That was a vision I was willing to work very hard for.

Jean, in addition to helping out in the shop when she could, also kept the books. We were working right there in the two-car garage behind the house, and we were up early every morning, getting a lot done every day. Nothing was a burden for Jean. Nothing. When I was in the middle of a fire escape project, sometimes I'd set it out and she'd paint it for me, or drill holes for me. Every day at some point, she'd come out and ask if there was something she could do, some way she could help. She was always there for me. Always.

I just brought in the money and gave it to her and she deposited it and paid the bills. I didn't even think about what we were saving or spending—as long as the jobs were covering costs and making me a good profit. And it felt so good to be busy. Every so often I thought about where I came from, the kind of subsistence living I grew up in, and it just made me want to keep working harder.

About a year or maybe eighteen months after I had left High Steel, Jean told me something I wasn't expecting.

"Steve, we don't have any debt, and we have $10,000 in the bank."

I just stared her. "You have got to be kidding."

She smiled and shook her head. And that was just the beginning. This was around 1962. I think that's when I got a clear vision for what this business could become, if we kept going in the right direction.

Steve is in the front row, dressed in black, and is in first grade at the
Black Horse School in Paradise, PA. It was a one-room schoolhouse
with grades 1-4 on the first floor and grades 5-8 on the second floor.
The Amish graduated from school after 8th grade. The teacher for
grades 1-4 was Pearl Brubaker.

Steve at age 18 working as a foreman building silos for J.C Snavely located in Landisville, PA.

Steve, during the Korean War, with Archie, his favorite dog.

Steve, during the Korean War, inside the compound.

Steve and his buddies having fun – stuffing Steve in the trash bin.

Steve with Army buddy, Jack Boshimi, who was from Philadelphia, PA.

Steve built this bar in the compound for the guys to use for exercise.
They didn't have any money so they created this for fun.

Steve was drafted into basic training with this group on October 24, 1952, and this picture was taken 10 days before they were discharged to return back to the States in October 1954. Steve is in the back row with his buddy, Jim Concuries, from McAdoo, PA.

Steve right after he returned from the Korean War.

Steve and Jean in March 1955 when they were dating. Jean was 18 and Steve was 23.

Steve returned from Aston, Wyoming in 1964 with his prize moose and outfits for everyone. Tammy was not born yet.

All four kids in our backyard at our newly built home in
Willow Street, PA in 1966.

A family portrait from 1969.
Back row: Patti, Steve Jr., Jean, Steve Sr.
Front row: Kurt, Tammy

Easter morning, 1970, on the front porch of the family's home
in Willow Street, PA.

Steve and his youngest daughter Tammy,
West Palm Beach, Florida, 1969.

First crane Steve ever bought.
It was 1972 and this was a **P&H** 40-ton, hydraulic crane.

Steve shooting skeet at Shorty Waters farm in New Providence, PA.

Steve with good friend, Nix Dagen, in 1958 when he took his first
hunting trip out west to Buffalo, Wyoming, to hunt mule deer and
antelope. Good friend, Ike Metzler was also on this trip. Steve saved up
for three years to go and it cost $350. They drove out from PA.

Amos H. Fisher, Steve's father, in 1976, sitting in his kitchen reading.

Steve, his brother Joe, sister Katie, and sister Susie, in Pinecraft,
Sarasota, Florida.

Jean's parents, Walter and Arlene Erb.

Jean and Steve at Super Bowl XV – Philadelphia Eagles vs Oakland
Raiders. Oakland linebacker, Rod Martin, intercepted Philadelphia
quarterback, Ron Jaworski three times for a Superbowl record.
Sadly, the Eagles lost.

Steve and Jean celebrating their 25th wedding anniversary in February, 1981.

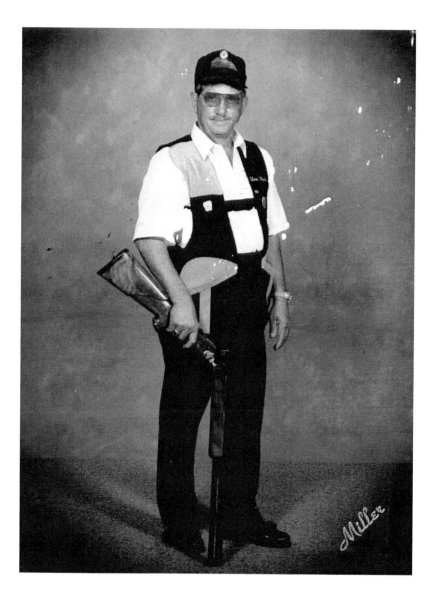

Steve's Skeet Shooting Hall of Fame Portrait. He was inducted in the Pennsylvania Skeet Shooting Hall of Fame in 1997.

Steve and Jean at a wedding in 1988.

Jean and Steve sitting at the Blue Mountain Cabin in Franklin County. They bought this cabin in 1974 and it is still enjoyed by the family today.

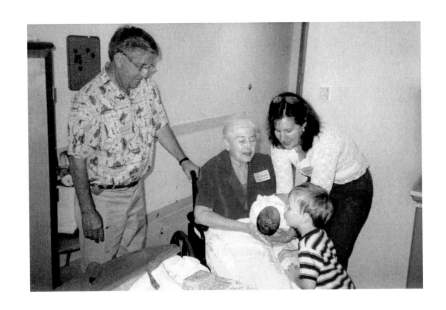

Jean meeting Caity Jean on July 26, 2004.
Steve with daughter Patti and grandson, Carson.

Steve with his children at Christmas, 2006, after losing Jean.

Steve and his best friend, Dave Anderson, at a member-guest golf
tournament in Sarasota in 1995.

Steve and his second wife Rosene Hoffer.

Chapter Eighteen
Mother's Passing

I had my own family by then, but I still stopped by the house on occasion to see Mom. And I often thought of the conversation I had with her before I left the Amish, when I was only fifteen or so, when I tried to prepare her for the day I would be leaving home. How we cried together.

But I didn't see her much; my own life was busy, and she and Dad were still Amish. The things we had in common hadn't increased as the years went on, and our paths didn't naturally cross very often.

Then she found out she had cancer, and that hurt. Even

if she hadn't always been able to be present, she was still my mother. She was still the one who had woken me up every morning to go do the chores and made meals for us. So, I started going by the house a little more often, and as the weeks passed, she kept getting sicker and sicker.

On one Saturday morning in February, when her cancer had her down and she was nearing the end, I decided to go by the farm and see her. By the time I arrived, she was already in a coma, and while I sat there beside her bed, she passed away. It was just me and Dad and a nurse there when it happened in that back room, the room she always took refuge in, the room where she often hid from the world in her sadness. For a little while, I just sat there and stared at her. I couldn't believe she was gone.

That was it.

My mom and I had a good relationship. I can't speak for the other children, but for me, she's what I would call a good mother. I'm sure there's a lot that went on at home after I left that I never heard about. I guess that's the way it goes, when you have such a large family, with so many years separating the oldest child from the youngest.

My mother was sixty-four years old when she died of cancer. By then, I was in the steel business and the welding business and things were going well for us. I was making good money, especially for a little Amish boy who hadn't gone to school beyond the eighth grade.

After my mother's funeral, which was a typical Amish affair, we were all sitting in my parents' house, and my dad was over on the couch with his head hanging down. I sat there for a long time looking at him, wondering why things had been the way they were with him. Why he was the way he was. And I thought, *I've got to do something for him.*

So, I drifted over to where he was and sat down beside him. Even as I sat down, I thought about what a rare occurrence it was to sit so near him, being that close. I had children of my own by then, and I just couldn't figure out why we had such a strained relationship. I didn't have trouble connecting with my young children, playing with them, or caring for them. Why had that been so hard for my dad?

"Dad," I said, hesitating, "do you need any help financially?"

I tried to say it quietly so that no one else in the room would hear. I really had no idea how he would respond. We didn't see each other that much in those days—I was busy with my business and family, and he was working steady as ever on the farm. No reaction would have surprised me. He could have been offended, or shocked, or relieved. But I felt like making the offer was something I needed to do. Something I wanted to do. I can't really explain it.

He hesitated a bit and leaned toward me. "I could use two thousand dollars," he said quietly. "Just for six months or so, to get me through."

I nodded. "Okay. Tomorrow I'll bring you a check, and you can pay your bills or whatever you need to do with it."

He nodded, and I sat there quietly for a few more minutes. I don't remember what happened after that. I don't think he said anything else, and I guess after a little while I stood up and walked away.

The next day, I drove to the home farm and gave him the

check and that was that. We barely spoke of it, and there was no expectation on my behalf on how quickly he would pay it back. To be honest, I didn't know if he would be able to. I had no idea what his financial situation was. But I didn't care, not really. I was just glad to give it to him.

About six months later, he paid me back. I don't remember the details of that, but I imagine he gave me a check one day when I stopped by the farm. I'm sure we didn't make a big deal about it. There was no conversation, and if he wouldn't have been able to pay me back, I wouldn't have gone asking him for it.

That's the way it was.

But I will say that it did go through my mind, how he had told me when I was sixteen years old that I shouldn't come to him for help if I needed it. I didn't feel spiteful about it or better than my dad in any way. It honestly just felt good to help him when he needed it. But still, you remember those things. I was thirty-three when I gave that money to my dad. Seventeen years had passed since he'd told me not to ask him for help.

I guess I had come a long way.

Chapter Nineteen
If Dad Did It Over Again

My dad died in 1988 at the age of ninety-two. Thirteen of his fifteen children survived into adulthood, and those thirteen children, over the span of forty years, had 69 grand-children. What an incredible family!

To be honest, though, my dad's death didn't have much of an impact on me. I guess whenever a parent dies, it leaves you a little quiet, but we never had much of a relationship, so his death didn't affect me. Not really. I went to the funeral and went to the graveside. I never held a grudge against my dad, even though he treated all of us boys unfairly. At least, that's how I saw it. It certainly wasn't a good way to raise sons.

But I also have come to a kind of understanding. I know he was trying to be strict—maybe he thought that's how you raised boys into men? And we were a handful, that's for sure. What else was he going to do with six boys, all of us full of piss and vinegar?

Sometime later, my brother-in-law Stevie Petersheim and I were chatting about something, and he said, "Your dad told me one time he wished he hadn't been so hard on you boys." I know Stevie wouldn't have said that unless it was true. "He told me that if he had to do it over again, he wouldn't have been so hard on you."

I was surprised to hear that my dad had said that, but thinking about it now, I'm sure it had to develop in his mind, a kind of regret that he wasn't closer to us, especially as we got older and became men and started out on our own lives. Of course, I'd rather have heard it straight from my dad, but it was still good to know he felt that way.

Like I said before: all of us boys were so full of energy— we brought the house down around us. How do you hold six rambunctious boys down? You can't. And me, well, I was told more than once by more than one person that I was the most rebellious of them all, and maybe I was and maybe I wasn't. I don't know.

That rebellion became my God-given gift, and as I got older it turned into an entrepreneurial spirit. I always, from as early as I can remember, wanted to do it on my own.

So, I guess Dad had his own regrets, just like I have a few of my own. I guess that's life.

Chapter Twenty
Growing the Business

In December 1965, we moved the family from the town of Rawlinsville to the town of Willow Street—yes, Willow Street was actually a town. I built a beautiful custom stone rancher-style home on a dead end street called Breezy Knoll Road. There were times I just could not believe it. On a separate lot down over the hill from where we built our home was a building owned by the Armstrong brothers of the now Armstrong World Industries. I approached them to see if we could rent it from them for our growing business, S.S. Fisher Welding Company. They said yes—another godsend.

I was in there for about a year when I landed a contract with the New Holland Machine Company building parts, and once I had that job, I needed a lot more room, so I went back to the Armstrong brothers and asked them to put an addition onto the building.

They weren't really into doing that—I guess they didn't want to spend the money—but they did come back with an interesting counter-offer.

"We don't want to do that, but we'll sell you the building," they told me.

I laughed. "I don't have enough money to buy a building," I said.

"You don't need any money," one of the brothers said, and he took me to an attorney, wrote up the papers, and told me to pay him as I could. I borrowed a little money to put the addition on, and we were all set.

We got busy doing work for New Holland Machine. They had a jig you'd put the parts in and weld them together, clean them up, and send them back. This went on for about fifteen months, five days a week plus half a day on Saturdays. I did well with it because I was on top of it all the time, constantly making sure our work was good and completed on time. We had a bunch of kids straight out of high school who were learning how to weld, and many of them took up the trade and ended up being welders for a long time. I've always been proud of that, being part of helping a young person start out in life with a valuable trade.

New Holland Machine liked the work we did and approached me about moving the company.

"We're moving our Lancaster office to Grand Island, Nebraska," they said. "We'd like you to move out there and do work for us in Nebraska.

Well, I had to think about that. It was a big account, worth a lot of money, but I had a very young family at home and felt established in Lancaster. What if I moved out there, where they would be my only customer, and they decided they didn't want me anymore? Then I'd really be stuck.

I decided not to do it. We stayed in Lancaster county.

After they moved, we lost that job but went on to do bigger and better things. We started doing contracts worth $50,000 to $100,000, and that gave me more confidence than ever. The jobs continued getting bigger and bigger, and then in 1974, I heard they were building a new courthouse in Lancaster, and I thought, *We could do the steel for that. We're ready for a big project.*

We put in a bid, and it turned out we were $25,000 lower than High Steel, my old employer. Sanford's son, Calvin, wasn't happy about our bid being that much lower than theirs, and he went into the city and told the project manager that "Fisher won't get that job done." At least, that's what I heard through the grapevine.

But they still gave us the job, and it was by far our biggest project to date.

When I heard what Calvin had said, I decided I was going to be the project manager and make certain there weren't any problems on the job. I went in just about every day, and we finished the Lancaster County Courthouse in 1975. I made $350,000 on that project alone, and that was the beginning of us taking on even bigger projects, like the Harrisburg Hospital.

One thing I want to mention here is that my dad, the one I never managed to have a conversation with when I was a kid, would sometimes come into the city and watch us work on that new courthouse. He'd just sit there on a bench, and he wouldn't even tell me when he came or when he left, but sometimes I'd be on the jobsite and I'd look over and there he was. Just watching.

That meant a lot to me.

Of course, he never said he was impressed or that he liked the building or that I was doing a good job. But the fact that he would take the time to come watch told me all that I needed to know.

In those days, we took on some huge projects, but we were able to make it happen. After that, I hired people smarter than me and just gave them a little guidance. At our peak, I had seven or eight people running the company with me.

We started in 1962 by building fire escapes as S.S. Fisher Welding Company, and by 1988 we had grown into Fisher Steel Corporation and were doing $20 million a year in sales with 100 employees. I may not have had a formal education, but I had a lot of good sense paired with ambition, and I guess if you put those two things together, you can make it work. Of course, I did a lot of learning on the job, and many days it felt like we were taking two steps forward and one step back, but we figured it out.

In those days, we used to have company Christmas parties, and we'd invite all the employees and their families. We invited my dad, too, and he'd come along and sit quietly in the fire hall where we had them. We paid some ladies to cook the meal, and the whole thing was a lot of fun. And I remember one of the times, when we had the Christmas party at the Rawlinsville fire hall, I sat down beside him, and he looked at me with a strange expression on his face and asked me a question.

"Are these all your workers?" I'm sure he probably asked me in Pennsylvania Dutch, and he didn't go any further. I told him, yes, all of them were my employees and their families, and he just frowned to himself and nodded. That was it. I could see his mind turning, calculating just how big the business had become. And again, I think he was proud of what I'd been able to accomplish. I hope he was.

I see Calvin High a lot these days, and he's become a good friend of mine. Later on, after the courthouse project, High Steel got into the bridge-building business, and they started leaning away from the structural work. They still needed structural steel for the warehouses they built, so they started giving me a lot of work at that point.

That's one thing you see as you get older—relationships mean a lot, and they make a big difference when you're trying to make it in the world.

Chapter Twenty-One
Buying Farms and Tough Times

Around the time we did the courthouse, I became interested in buying the farm across the street from our shop. I played golf with a guy named John Way, and he was involved in real estate. We were good buddies.

"I'd like to buy that farm across the street," I told him. "Do you have any connections?"

He said he'd look into it, and eventually we approached the owner, agreed on a price, and they were willing to let me pay them a certain amount each quarter until it was paid off, which took two or three years.

I bought that farm—that's where our shop is now—and we used it as a yard to store larger equipment and materials. We also used it as a landfill and made some money from that. Plus, at the top of the hill, I put in a small development and built twenty-five to thirty houses, and that was a good income.

That was in 1972, and things were really hopping. I accumulated a fair amount of money over the next ten years or so. During that time, I told Jean, "It isn't going to stay this way. When President Carter gets out of here, and we get another president, things are going to change."

The thing about Jean, she was always willing to take a risk, and she trusted me. She always told me to do whatever I thought was best for the family.

By the time the 80s rolled around, business slowed down a bit. Interest rates soared to 17 percent, and it felt like no one was buying anything to speak of. If you wanted to buy something, anything really, you could get it for thirty cents on the dollar, as long as you had cash to pay for it and didn't have to borrow money from the banks.

I had decent cash flow by then, and I figured the economy wouldn't stay down like that forever, so I spent most of the free cash I had within the span of eighteen months. The farm I live on today, I bought during that time for $350,000 in 1980. Then I had an opportunity to buy a shopping center in town for $400,000, so I did, and we added some offices to it.

Not much later, there was another farm for sale in Christiana, Pennsylvania, a 120-acre farm, and I told Jean I was going to go to the auction and just see what happened. I went there and I bought it for $320,000.

I walked into the house later that afternoon. "Well, Jean," I said. "You own another farm."

"Oh," she said. "In that case, I want to see it."

Later that day we drove down to the farm and walked around the property. The farm had two streams running through it—they sort of came down and then combined into one stream on the other side of the road. She saw those two streams and thought we should call it Twin Brook Acres. That was her contribution, and that's what we called it.

We developed the land on that farm, and at the end we had thirty-five acres remaining. I had always been interested in having a vineyard, so I took a sample of the soil up to Harrisburg, and it came back ideal for grapes. There was a guy helping me out at the landfill at the time, so I took him out for lunch and asked him if he wanted to be a partner with me in the vineyard, and he agreed. After five years, I sold out my interest in the company to him, and to this day it's still a vineyard: Twin Brook Vineyard.

I guess that's something I learned early on—if you had an opportunity, you had to take it instead of just sitting back and thinking about it. Fortunately, Jean was on the same page. She was always up for the next challenge, the next risk, and that's pretty much how we lived our life together.

By the end of the 80s, I was paying $300,000 to $400,000 a year in taxes, and my CPA said we needed to make some adjustments because they felt it was too much to be paying out, so we decided to put up a shop across the road with all the latest equipment. We spent all the money I had plus whatever I could get from the bank to put it together.

Of course, right after that we ran into a slow time for the business. I had a tough time pulling out of that.

To be honest, I wasn't really sure what I was going to do. We still had our original shop, which I had sold to the four kids two years prior. They had started Steel Fab Enterprises in 1988, a miscellaneous metals business, and because it was established, that meant they were protected while I did everything I could to save the big shop.

There was an African-American guy named Steve Powell working for me at the time, my head of Human Resources, and when we ran into these hard times, he went out and borrowed $3 million through a minority loan. He bought my assets and kept the team in place, buying me out. He rented the shop from me and ran it for about twenty years, very successfully, at which point he got cancer, and by then the kids were in a place to buy the assets back from him. We are running that business today.

If Steve wouldn't have been able to put that money together, we would have lost everything except the building to bankruptcy. As it was, we were on the verge. Fortunately, I was able to sell the equipment to him and use some of the money to pay my creditors. It really helped me out of what could have been a humiliating situation.

Still, the headlines in the paper about my business going under were painful, and so was the fact that I had to sell what I had worked so hard to start. My daughter Tammy recently told me she never remembers me being more distraught than I was in those days. It was extremely stressful and hard for me.

We had to auction off our farm, too, but it didn't sell. Jean and I had to sell a lot of the personal things we owned that had value—land and commercial property. I looked at my life and wondered what was happening. I had worked so hard, diversified, and then watched as it all seemed to be going down the drain. It was hard to imagine life ever getting better.

Of course, during that time, Jean was awesome and encouraging.

But, you know, I bounced back. Fortunately, I had been passing the smaller work onto the kids at the original shop, so they were well-established by the time I had to get rid of the big shop. In a way, that business ended up being a real blessing to all of us.

And since I didn't lose the building, I still had the rental income every month from that. That was significant.

If I ever lost any sleep during all of my years in business, it was during that time. It was hard to imagine losing everything I had worked so hard for. But these things happen, and you just have to keep going. The kids and I worked together, and we managed to work it out.

Chapter Twenty-Two
Our Family

Jean and I started having children soon after we were married. Stephen was born in 1956; Patti in 1957; Kurt in 1960; and Tammy came along in 1965. Four children. It was a good-sized family, perfect as far as I was concerned, and much more manageable than the thirteen siblings I was part of growing up.

I guess my approach to being a father was a direct reaction to how my father parented us. From the beginning, I was determined not to be that way—quiet, disconnected, unemotional. I wanted to communicate with my children and show them all the love I could possibly put together.

But, you know, Jean was the spark for that. She was the spark of love in the family, and I followed her example. Without Jean, there's no telling what kind of parent I might have been, but with her there to show me what affection looked like, it really helped me become the kind of father I wanted to be.

I already told you how in 1965 we built a house up on the hill behind the shop, right there in Willow Street. It was a beautiful home with a nice big swimming pool. We dedicated the basement as a recreation area for the kids and their friends. We had all kinds of games down there—a pool table, Ping-Pong, air hockey, darts, and a big area with couches and a television. Our house became the center of attraction for the whole neighborhood. Everyone spent time there because we had the pool and the rec room. Whenever I had time, I was right there with them, in the middle of it all.

I always preferred that all the kids in the neighborhood come to our house. I'd rather know where my kids were and have everyone else there as well than have my kids running all over the countryside without me knowing what they were up to or who they were spending time with.

Jean and I would often sit upstairs watching television, and there would be so much commotion downstairs. We could hear all the kids running around and screaming and laughing down in the basement, and Jean would turn to me. "Don't you think you should go down and see what those kids are doing?"

"No," I'd say. "I'm sure it's fine."

The next morning, Jean would send Tammy (who was much younger) down to the basement to see how many teenagers had spent the night so she'd know how much breakfast to make. Tammy would come back up and report, "There are nine kids down there, Mom."

"Well, then set the table for our family plus nine," Jean

would say.

And after Tammy set the table, she'd go downstairs and round everyone up. They'd all come upstairs and sit around our table for a family breakfast, and I could tell that some of them had never done that before. Some of their families never took the time to share a meal together. For some, I guess it was a little awkward, but it wasn't long before they had fallen in love with Jean, because she was like a mom to everyone.

That's just the kind of lady Jean was. She wanted everyone to feel at home, to have a home. There were kids who showed up who came from some tough situations, and even times when one of those kids would move in with us for a while, just to give them some space to get their life back together.

We had motorcycles and horses and snowmobiles. We went on vacation. But we worked hard, too, and that made the fun times all the sweeter.

I only had a few things that I was particular about. The chores needed to be done, and done right. If I gave the kids a curfew, I expected them to be home at that time. If they were a minute late, then we had a hard conversation. And everyone was expected to be at the dinner table at five thirty sharp. They had to pay attention to the time, because I wasn't going to go chasing them all over the countryside and gather them in for dinner. That was one of the few things I didn't have tolerance for.

Besides those things, I just let them go, let them be kids.

Today, I really enjoy my kids. I have four of the greatest children a person could ever ask for. That's one thing that hasn't changed in all these years.

Chapter Twenty-Three
Hunting and Skeet Shooting

When it came to hunting, when Jean and I first got married, we didn't have a lot of money lying around, so if I wanted to go hunting, I had to save up. I had never hunted much when I lived on the farm as a kid. It was after I got back from the service that I took an interest in it, and it took a few years before the business was successful enough to pay for my trips and allow me the time to do it.

It took a few years of me saving a little here, a little there, and by 1958, I had enough saved up to go hunting out west for the first time. The whole trip cost $350, and four of us guys took off for Buffalo, Wyoming, going after mule deer. It ended up being quite the trip, ten days I'll never forget, and each of us brought back a mule deer and an antelope. That was the beginning of my love of hunting. I really enjoyed it and thought I needed to do more of it.

In 1967, we went to Wyoming again, to the town of Afton this time, and we hired an outfitter who took us by horseback up to around an elevation of seven thousand feet, right at the timberline, and that's where we hunted. There was an outpost camp there with tents and a corral for the horses. We had all applied for permits to hunt trophy mule deer and Shiras moose, and while we all got permits to hunt mule deer, I was the only one lucky enough to get a moose permit—they only gave out a certain number of those every year, for that particular moose.

While we were up there, on the second or third day, it started snowing, and it was one of the most beautiful things I've ever seen. And it was cold. Because of the snow, we couldn't get out early that morning. I guess there was about a foot of snow on the ground, and I started getting cabin fever, so I suggested we go out and scout around to see if we could find anything in the snow with our binoculars.

We got out there and saw an animal pretty far up, so I got out my scope and there it was.

A nice Shiras moose.

The Shiras moose can be found throughout southwest Canada and in various places in the United States, and while it's the smallest of the three kinds of moose found in North America, it's certainly not small—the bulls can weigh as much as 1,200 pounds! They don't like swamps and tend to stay in higher elevations, high up, right at the timberline.[1]

It took us a couple of hours to circle around and cross over at that elevation—the going was tough. We came up over a hill and got to the top, and the guide who was with me stopped his horse right away.

"There he is," he told me, taking the reins off my horse. I got down, took my gun, and climbed over the edge of the hill. And right there he was. I put that moose in my sights, pulled the trigger, and down he went.

By the time this was all said and done, it was around three p.m., and we still had to gut the moose, trim it out, and quarter it. We didn't get much of that done before dark, and the guide said we needed to head back to camp. We had to leave the moose there, not knowing what would happen overnight.

We left, and the next morning we got our gear together—four horses and a donkey. When we arrived, I was so relieved to see that nothing had bothered the moose overnight. We put a quarter of the moose on each horse and the head on the donkey (the horses don't like horns and wouldn't have willingly carried the head).

We got back late that day, and it was a good tale to tell.

Everyone in the hunting party got their elk, and it turned out that I shot a record moose, the fourteenth largest ever shot, and it was listed in the Boone and Crocket book where they keep hunting records. I think by now it's down to about the twenty-

---

[1] "Differences between Canadian Moose and Shiras Moose!" Total Outdoor Adventures, accessed January 15, 2021, https://toaltd.com/differences-canadian-moose-shiras-moose/.

sixth biggest moose ever shot, because a period of time has passed, and there have been bigger ones.

But I did a lot of that kind of hunting in those days.

I started skeet shooting in 1966. I had taken a real liking to guns and hunting, and in 1966, a friend, Chet Flowers, took me along to a skeet shoot one weekend. We went up to a place they had in Trexlertown, PA, and from the first shot, I got hooked. I just loved it. From then on, we had a place down in New Providence where I practiced a lot.

The next year, I joined the National Skeet Shooting Association (NSSA). Two years later, I became a AA-shooter across the board, a top-class shooter, and I started going to tournaments all across the country.

To reach that level, you have to practice a lot, and you need to have determination in your practice. I guess it's like becoming a professional at any sport—you really have to work at it. After I joined the NSSA, every time I did a shoot, it was registered in San Antonio, Texas, at the NSSA central office. They keep track and develop an average for you, and that's what is used to place you in a class. It starts with D, and then as you improve, you move up through C, B, A, and finally AA.

I became a AA-shooter by getting my average high enough, up to 97.5 out of every 100 shots. I had a higher average with 12-gauge than I did with the smaller gauges, but I was still very competitive with the smaller ones, because I was a smaller guy and the large guns would beat me up if I shot them enough.

I was there with the best shooters, and the tournaments

really got my adrenaline going. You had to shoot a perfect 100 out of 100 to get to the final, sudden-death shoot-offs. Whenever I see golfers today, and they get into the final day of a big tournament, I can see their adrenaline rushing, their concentration focusing. There's nothing else on their mind apart from that next shot—if they can keep their mind clear, they'll win.

That's how I was when I was skeet shooting in a tournament. I couldn't think of anything else. It was all about the next shot.

I remember one of my earliest tournaments, just when I was starting to peak as a shooter, and it was in West Palm Beach. Jean and I would go down there every year to visit one of her aunts, and every year I would go to the skeet-shooting tournament that took place during that time of year. That was the first weekend that I shot 100 for 100 with a 12-gauge—it was amazing.

So, I advanced to the sudden-death finals with three other guys. We just kept exchanging shots, one after the other, and all of us kept hitting. No misses. We went five boxes deep, and after 125 additional sudden-death shots, I finally outlasted the competition and won the tournament. It was a pretty neat moment.

Just as I finished shooting, who came walking out of the audience but Molly and Earl Clark from Lancaster—they owned Dutch Wonderland at the time, and they had a home down in West Palm Beach. They came out and met me there and congratulated me on the win. It was great.

We accomplished quite a bit in the skeet-shooting world during those years. Eight years in a row, we won the state championship. I traveled to Puerto Rico five years in a row and won in shoot-outs. We won the PA five-man team championships four years out of five, and I won the 12-gauge title.

By 1981, I stopped shooting competitively—it was a real grind, and my reflexes weren't nearly as good as they were when I was younger. I just couldn't beat those young guys anymore in the shoot-outs. I could still go 100 for 100 in the regular rounds, but I just couldn't go far enough into the sudden-death rounds anymore.

I quit shooting and spent more time golfing.

One night in August, 1997, a couple of the boys came along and invited me up to the Pennsylvania state skeet-shooting dinner. I didn't really know what it was all about, but I showed up, and it was good to see everyone.

They invited me up front, and that's when they told me I was being inducted into the PA Skeet Shooters Hall of Fame. Every year there are five shooters nominated, and then from those five, one is chosen by the Hall of Fame board.

It felt good. I didn't know if I'd ever get selected or not. It was a big accomplishment, icing on the cake.

And Jean was with me the whole time. She always traveled with me for tournaments. She was always there.

In the late 70s, my skeet-shooting friend, a plumber named Harry Stilwell, decided he and I should go fishing, so we booked a trip to Alaska for salmon. On that first trip, we fished for chum salmon, sockeye, and king.

We did that trip four years in a row, and it was just amazing. But a few years later, we decided to go for the Arctic

Char, which survives only in the tundra. So, we flew into Edmonton, Alberta, and from there we flew north in a float plane, 360 miles above the Arctic Circle. What an inspiring trip—I've never seen anything like it in my life.

The float plane only held six or eight passengers, and it could only land on water, which is a good thing because up there in the tundra, during that time of year, the surface is 50 percent water. It was July, during their six weeks of summer, and all the ice had melted off the tundra.

We lived up there for ten days, and it never got dark, and we fished for char.

During those days, if you took a shovel and stuck it down into the dirt, once you got down eight inches or so, you'd hit solid ice. The dirt was the richest top soil you can imagine, and the flowers grew so fast during that short summer you could almost see them growing. After five or six days, the entire tundra was carpeted with flowers. We had the pleasure of seeing it— absolutely beautiful.

We stayed there for ten days and lived on the fish we caught. I never knew in my life there was anything as beautiful or amazing as the tundra.

It's been a good life. I've gotten to do things I never would have dreamed of when I was a little Amish boy.

Chapter Twenty-Four
Losing Jean

In 1983, Jean was in the shower when she dropped the soap. And after that, she would always say it was a God thing that she fumbled with the soap that morning, because otherwise, she may not have put her hand to her breast in that particular spot and felt the tiny, hard lump under her skin. She didn't do anything about it for three months because she didn't want to interfere with our trip to the Holy Lands. She didn't tell anyone about it, not even me. That was just like her.

When we got back, she went into the doctor and was diagnosed with breast cancer. It was hard news to bear. She was forty-eight years old, and the cancer was in her lymph nodes. She did chemo, a lot of it, and radiation, and then she had a lumpectomy.

I decided at that point that something had to change. I was away from the house too much. So I got all of my key people together at the shop and sat them down.

"My wife has cancer," I explained. "I'm going to spend more time with her, as much time as I can, and you guys are going to have to run the company. I've got you all tuned in pretty well to how I like things run. Now you have to do it without me."

After that, Jean and I traveled down to Florida and bought a villa in the Palm Aire Country Club community. We spent about three months down there the first winter after her diagnosis.

When she was forty-nine, they found another lump, and it was benign, and then at fifty, they found another lump, which was cancerous.

I scheduled a lunch with her oncologist without telling the rest of the family. I wanted to ask him a few questions, face-to-face. We met, and at some point during our time together, I said, "Now look, I have a young family. I need to know what's going to happen so that I can plan ahead if I need to." I paused. "How long does she have?"

He looked at me for a moment. "You're asking me, and I can respect your position. I can't tell for sure, but the way I see it, she has five years to live."

This was around 1986, three or four years after her initial diagnosis.

Oh, my God, I thought. *I'm not ready for this.*

Jean did another whole round of chemo and radiation, and that round was hard on her. She was a go-getter and a hard worker, but the treatment really knocked her down. She slept on the couch a lot, and it took her about five years before she really had her energy back.

After this round of treatment, they put her on this drug called Tamoxifen, an estrogen blocker. Patti went with her to those treatments, and as soon as the chemo was in her veins, she'd start throwing up. But she never complained.

She was on Tamoxifen for thirteen years, and she never said one thing about the side effects bothering her. No complaints whatsoever. But at the end of those thirteen years, one of her doctors told her she didn't need to take it anymore, because it was only effective for about ten years. By that time we had long surpassed the predicted five year mark, and we were feeling grateful.

She stopped taking it, and within six months, she had cancer in her bones. She was sixty-three years old at that point. The pain started in her hip, and eventually she would get a hip replacement. Then she had pain in her knee, and another spot of cancer showed up there. She started taking chemo pills, and this went on for years.

When she was sixty-eight, she went to the doctor just before we left for Florida. It seemed like every time we were about to leave for Florida, the doctor would bring up something about her health or her cancer, but she'd say she didn't care.

"I'm going to Florida," she would always say.

So the doctor called down to Florida ahead of us and set up some appointments for her.

When we returned home to Lancaster after spending the winter in Florida, she went into the hospital yet again, and my daughter Patti, who was living in Montana at the time, called Jean. She didn't think Jean sounded like herself, so she called my other daughter Tammy, who still lived in the Lancaster.

"You need to get to the hospital," Patti told Tammy. "I think they've got Mom on too many pain meds. She doesn't sound right."

But it turned out that she was talking like that because she had two brain tumors, one in each hemisphere, so they suggested doing a "gamma knife procedure," which involved putting a helmet on her that had two tiny holes in it, allowing them to focus radiation directly on the tumors. They said this could get her two more years, so she opted to try it. Patti took her in every day for her treatments, and this went on for two or three weeks.

One morning, Patti was getting her ready, putting on Jean's lipstick, when Patti noticed Jean's mouth was drooping and her eye was twitching. After an MRI, the doctor called Patti in and said the cancer had spread to her spinal fluid, and it wouldn't be long.

The family gathered in our garage and we filled everyone in on what was going on—Jean hadn't yet heard the news about the cancer being in her spinal fluid, and so we told her. That was the second time in twenty years I saw her cry about her cancer— once when she first found out at age forty-eight, and then when she discovered, at sixty-eight,the cancer was in her spinal fluid.

At one point, Tammy leaned in close to Jean. "I can't do this without you, Mom. You can't leave me."

"Sure you can," Jean replied. "I have given you everything you need to do this without me, you just have to believe in yourself."

The year before, Tammy and her husband Jim told us they had decided they weren't having any more children and that Jim was going to have a vasectomy. This would mean their son would be an only child. I thought that was the worst thing they could do to him. Jean was devastated as well, insisting that they have more children.

Tammy got a little defensive and told us she was thirty-eight years old, and it was a decision that she and Jim could make.

"I'm sorry it's not matching up with what you've been hoping for," she told us.

"Well," Jean said. "I'm going to stay up all night and pray that you still get pregnant."

Tammy just shook her head.

Jim went ahead with the surgery, and six months later, Tammy found out she was pregnant. When she sent the photo of the sonogram to Jean, Jean was ecstatic. That baby and Jean had a special connection from the very beginning. I guess Jean felt she had prayed this little girl into existence.

Fast-forward to that moment in the garage when Jean was told the cancer had spread to her spinal fluid. Tammy was eight months pregnant and had a C-section scheduled a month from then. Jean was bound and determined to make it until her granddaughter was born. She did not want to die until meeting the baby who she had prayed so hard for.

"How are you?" I'd ask Jean. "Are you okay? You seem worse."

"Why are you worried?" she'd reply in a weak voice. "I'm going to see Tammy's baby. You don't have to worry about that."

Meanwhile, Tammy kept trying to convince the doctors to

move her C-section up a little earlier, and we were all hoping Jean could make it until then. Eventually, the doctor's said they couldn't move it any closer.

"This baby is coming out on July 26 and don't ask again," her doctor exclaimed.

Jean would look at Tammy with the calmest eyes, as sick as she was, and tell her, "I don't know why you're worrying. I'm going to see Caity Jean enter the world."

On July 26, 2004, our granddaughter Caity Jean was born. And Jean was able to meet her. It was one of the last, most beautiful things Jean did.

That moment, when Jean met Caity Jean, it was spiritually divine—beyond special; a moment Jean felt responsible for through prayer early on, then through grace later on. Before her suffering, then amid her suffering, she somehow knew that she and Caity Jean would see each other face-to-face. We wheeled Jean into the room and it was like having a front-row seat to the blessed circle of life. As she held that newborn baby, just a few hours old, they were strangely similar, at opposite ends of life— one entering the world and one preparing to exit the world. They were both exhausted, they were both curious of one another, and they were both very dependent. They were simultaneously surrendering fully to their given moments—while those moments were vastly different, they were remarkably the same. The whole family was there in the room, but for a moment it was all about those two, just Jean and the baby. Tammy has said that when Jean held Caity Jean close, in that God-given moment, she weaved something into that little girl that was just between the two of them, something divinely special.

The moment felt deep and spiritually intentional . . . and just like that . . . it was gone. Jean had met the baby. That was the one thing she had been holding on for and was now accomplished. When she got home that night, she laid down, and I knelt beside her ear and said, "Jean, what did you think of little Caity Jean?"

"Oh," she whispered, so weak she could barely talk. "She is *so* precious."

That was the last thing Jean ever said.

She just kind of closed her eyes, and she didn't really open them again. When Tammy got out of the hospital just a few days later, she brought Caity Jean over to the house and laid her in the crook of Jean's arm, by then, Jean was peaceful and quiet, not responding.

Patti sat with Jean through those last days, and I was so glad she could do that. I did my thing on the farm, distancing myself. Sometimes I sat with Jean, but mostly it was just too hard for me to see her, to be reminded that she was leaving me. I kept thinking back through all of those years, how she had stood by me and every crazy idea I ever had, how she had always encouraged me, and how she had taught me about love and affection. I couldn't imagine life without her.

Patti slept beside her every night—I don't think she had ever been around someone who was dying.

I was outside when Jean died, and Patti came out and got me, told me to come in the house.

"She's gone," Patti said, weeping. I started sobbing, and I went over to her, tried to adjust the way she was lying on the bed. I was just beside myself. I just couldn't believe that someone who had been such a lively person could lay there so quiet.

Jean died on August 3rd, 2004.

There was never anyone like her. I'm a different person because of her.

The girls put Jean's funeral together, and it was absolutely beautiful. They did a wonderful job. But it was exhausting—there were so many people who wanted to come through the line, and it just seemed to go on and on forever. After the first four hundred people came through, the funeral director declared an intermission and we took a break. But everyone just remained in line waiting, while we went away for an hour.

We came back for the second half, and another three hundred people went through the line. So many people were touched by her life. I think it was pretty amazing for our kids to see that, and it does leave you wondering what it takes to touch so many lives the way she did.

It seemed just about everyone who came through had something wonderful to say about her. They'd lean in and hug us and tell us a story of how she changed their life. This person and this person and this person . . . just over and over again, story after story, and I started to understand how Jean hadn't just impacted her own family's life—she had played a huge part in our community, for many decades.

Jean's funeral service was the day after the viewing, and Pequea Brethren in Christ Church was packed full. It was a beautiful celebration, but all of us were just so sad. I wanted to try to celebrate Jean's life, but she had been the hub of everything—for her to simply be gone, absent from the festivities—it just brought an uninvited feeling of emptiness. How would we carry on without her?

Sitting at the front of the church with us was Tammy's little baby, only a week old. I just kept looking over at the baby, feeling so sad that Jean wouldn't be around to see her grow up. We were lost. I was lost.

After the viewing, after the funeral, after everything was cleaned up and the hall was cleared and the pictures were put away, after everyone had gone back to their own homes and families, I went home. Patti came with me. It was one of the hardest things in my life, just the two of us in the house, without Jean. I hadn't been without her for forty-eight years.

We sort of wandered around the empty house for a bit, and then we went to sleep. Patti went upstairs and climbed into bed, and I sat on the couch and covered myself with a blanket. We didn't even change out of our funeral clothes. We were so devastated and sad and exhausted.

I consider myself to be a patient person, and I'm not that emotional, but when I went back to Florida and walked into that beautiful villa that she had turned into a home, it was hard. It took me several years to work through that sadness and loneliness. During the first year, I had to keep telling myself over and over again that this is a different way of life. I had to adjust.

There were so many things the two of us enjoyed doing together, just us. We had season tickets to the Philadelphia Phillies, and we always had the television on, watching sports together. We went to four Super Bowls, and every Sunday we watched football together. Even when Jean was dying, she wanted the Phillies on the television in the background.

When we were younger, we played tennis. We enjoyed

each other, and she always came to my skeet shooting tournaments. She was always right up front, and whenever I made it into a shoot-out, I knew she'd be right there, watching.

We played games, too, and we were very competitive. When we got older, we played almost every night, any game that involved only two people. We'd have a cocktail and play a game.

So things were dark in those days after she died, no doubt, and I had to fight off depression. The evenings were the worst, when we would normally be sitting at the table playing a game and talking. Going to bed alone was the saddest part of my day.

I tried to keep very busy, flying out to Montana to stay with Patti and Gary while they built their ranch, and those days were full, and sometimes I found I could forget about my sadness, at least for a short period of time. Sometimes I'd stay out there for a few weeks at a time, and that was good for me, gave me a place to go. Gary kept me busy from daylight to dark every day, and the busyness was good for me. We worked on his first building there, a shop that was about 100 feet long by 40 feet wide, and once that was built, he turned a corner of it into living space. They had a kitchen with a grill, and Patti made it work. Some years later, they built a house.

For a long time, my life was simply me trying to stay busy so that I could forget about Jean, and about how much I had lost. But you can't live your life that way, not forever.

Chapter Twenty-Five
Starting Again

After Jean passed away, I went to Florida for two winters by myself. Every single morning when I woke up, I was lonely. I had become so used to having Jean around, laughing and talking, that without her, life felt very sad and quiet. I woke up every morning and took a nice long walk and then came back and made myself some breakfast. I didn't go out to restaurants much for breakfast because I liked my own cooking.

But one morning, I woke up and thought, I'm going out. I'm not cooking. I went to a place called First Watch, walked in the door, and there were ten women sitting around a table, all of them talking and having a fine time. I knew about half of them, and they invited me to join them at their table for breakfast.

Of those ten women, the one who sat directly across from

me caught my eye. Her name was Rosene Hoffer, and she was from Lititz, PA.

We were all there for a long time, and at one point, Rosene got up and went to the restroom, so I asked the lady beside me for Rosene's phone number. She gave it to me and later, without me knowing about it, she told Rosene I had asked for her number and might give her a call.

Well, I didn't call for six or seven months.

When I finally did call her, she played hard to get. I had to call her about five times until I finally got a date, and then I charmed her. We dated a little over a year, and we got married in 2009.

I'll be honest with you—I wondered if I was doing the right thing. I had such a wonderful life with Jean. Should I be getting married again? Could it be as good as it was before? I finally decided, yeah, I was going to do it. I was going to ask her to marry me. Because you just don't know what the future holds.

Rosene and I got married, and it was the right decision.

We've now been married for over ten years, and while I never thought about what it would be like to have a blended family, I have been grateful to get to know her daughters and their children. They have all been a blessing in my life in so many ways.

Chapter Twenty-Six
Things Keep Changing

I go back quite a ways now. I'm almost ninety years old, and that's a hard thing to believe sometimes. When I was a youngster here in Lancaster County, we never got out much—I can only tell you what I experienced during that time, during those years I was alive in the 30s, 40s, and 50s.

And I know I left the Amish, but I still think they're a wonderful and fascinating people. I've seen a lot of places, and Lancaster county is right up there as far as I'm concerned when it comes to beauty. The Amish own almost all the farms around here—all the farms around my house are owned by the Amish, except for one. That's why Lancaster is still such a beautiful place, because the Amish buy the farms and make them beautiful. And, for the most part, they don't sell their farms off for development

—with the money they accumulate, they buy more farms. The Amish are one of the main reasons the Lancaster countryside has remained so preserved, so beautiful.

In 1980 when I moved into the farm where I live now, there weren't any Amish around me. None. Now, you can't buy a farm because the Amish pay top dollar. Some time ago, I went to three sales with a friend of mine who was looking to buy a farm and acquire some land.

We always had a price in mind, but I warned him ahead of time. "Be prepared," I said. "You're not going to buy these farms. I'm sorry."

"What? Why not? What do you mean?"

I just shook my head. "You're not. You'll see."

One of the places we looked at in the early 80s was 135 acres, and he said he would set his top price at $750,000. I agreed that was a sensible price to pay. Well, the auction started at $700,000 and sold for just under a million dollars to an Amish buyer. That's why all the farms around us are owned by Amish farmers. And they're good people, good neighbors. I wouldn't choose to make it any different than it is.

Chapter Twenty-Seven
This Life I've Been Given

In 2019, my sister Annie seemed to be in her last days, and she told someone, "I want to see my brother Steve," so I went in to visit her. I was there for an hour or two—she was very weak and didn't say much. It was really something to think about all we had been through together, how we had grown up in that same house with our mom and dad so many years before.

I got ready to leave, and when I did, I bent down and whispered in her ear, "Now, when you get to heaven, you wash Jesus' feet, and I'll come up and dry them."

She got a smile on her face. She was really sweet. A wonderful sister.

I have a good friend named Dave Anderson, who I met in 1965, and he's been a big part of my life. When he got out of college, he moved into a house next door to us in Willow Street. He had no money, so he started selling insurance.

He and his wife had a son named Kurt, the same age as our Kurt, and the two boys became fast friends. In fact, our son walked over to visit them when they first moved in, and he came running back, all excited because "The people next door have a boy named Kurt! Same age as me, and the same name!"

They became friends and even went to college together, wrestled on the same team. Kurt Anderson was Kurt's best man.

Dave and I played a lot of golf together through the years, all over the country. We went to Miami for a week and also played out at Phoenix. We're both still members at the same golf club, and we have played a lot of gin rummy together.

We've also both lost our wives, so we helped each other through that. Dave Anderson is a good guy, and a great friend.

Almost all of my brothers and sisters are gone now. It's a strange feeling, when I think back to all of us growing up at the farm with my parents, the hard days we lived through, the fun times we had. It seems like a million years ago.

I did a lot with my brother Joe as the kids got older. I spent quite a lot of time with him in the last twenty years of his life, especially after he lost his wife Melinda. We'd just sit there and talk about the Fisher family, going way back. He had some interesting stories.

Joe stayed Old Order Amish until he died, living on the

original farm. He was so peaceful. If he needed something from the "real world," he'd always call me and ask how things worked.

It's been a good life. I had a wonderful wife in Jean, who taught me how to love, and then Rosene came along and she's been a loving wife and companion to me. I've always said I have four of the best children in the world, and now grandchildren and great-grandchildren, too.

If I were to describe each of my children in one word, the word I would choose for Steve would be "loyal." He was a loyal son to me, a loyal husband who has been married for forty-plus years, and a loyal father. That's the theme of his life—from the time he was a little boy, he paid attention to me, wanted to be like me, and turned out just the way I would have wanted.

Patti's word, actually two words, would be strong-willed and persevering. She's never been interested in taking the easy path, but she was always able to get through the hard times. She came through everything successfully. When I told her she was going to be the president of the business, she said, "Dad, I don't know how to do that." I told her she could do it. Just do it. And she went in there, in the dark, and found her way. She's been like that all her life. She's always found the open door.

For Kurt, I'd say "honest." A man of his word. A fun-loving guy to be around, and everyone loves him. I mean, everyone. And he would give the shirt off his back to a stranger who needed it. Kurt is a giving, big-hearted man. He's much like his mother. But most of all, I'd say he's honest.

Then there's Tammy, and my word for her is "vivacious."

Dorothy High was the first person to call her mother Jean vivacious, and that was so true—if we were playing cards in three different rooms, you knew which room Jean was in. And Tammy is just like that, too. When she gets into a room, it lights up.

These wonderful children. What else could a man want?

Life goes on. It does. It just keeps going on. Someday, I won't be around, but life will keep going.

I'm so thankful for the life I've been given.

The following four sections are written by Steve and Jean's children, from youngest to oldest.

Tammy

There can be a lot of different experiences of family within the same family. I've seen that in the family life my dad describes versus the way some of his siblings describe their growing-up years, and I've experienced it myself. I was the youngest of the four of us, and there were nine years between my oldest brother and me. Perhaps our perspectives are different because life is about constant change in people and places, or perhaps it's because we are just different in the way we perceive things. Either way, I think those differences lent themselves to different childhoods.

The different experiences among me and my older siblings

weren't just financial. We did have more money as I grew up, but Dad was also more relaxed by then. He had his nose to the grindstone pretty hard when my oldest brother was born, but by the time I came along, his dream was coming alive, and he was more relaxed.

The earliest memory I have of my dad was him tucking me into bed, something he did every night. One of my windows had a clear view of the moon, and we'd pull back the curtain and look at the moon together. I'm fifty-five now, and I look at the moon differently because of these memories. And it connects me with my dad.

After we looked at the moon, Dad would tell me I was safe, that he'd take care of me, and I had nothing to be afraid of. I believed it, because in my eyes as a child, he was big and mighty. There was a strength that came through what he said. There was something so cool about having a dad who made me feel safe.

If I had to sum up my dad Steve, the thing that I've always said about him is that he said what he meant and he meant what he said. There was this incredible level of consistency when it came to my dad, and I can't ever remember a time when he looked at me and said something he didn't mean. So I never had any doubt, and I always knew what my boundaries were—not that we kids didn't occasionally cross those boundaries when he wasn't looking, but we always knew what the results would be if we got caught. That was the one thing we never had to wonder about.

Now that I think about it, though, my dad was always very clear about something else: he loved my mother. You never had to wonder about that, either. They were best friends, and they had so many things in common. They both loved sports, and they had season tickets to the Philadelphia Phillies for thirty years. They attended games a lot all through my growing-up years. They also loved football, and just about every Sunday during football season, you would find them sitting in the living room watching it together, shouting at the television, both of them totally into it. They went to a number of Super Bowls as well. My mom was fun, she was always happy and laughed a lot. I could count on that. In fact, that is how I would find her at festivals or parties or in stores—I would wait and listen and without fail, within a few minutes, I would hear her hearty laugh sounding through the crowed, and it always led me straight to her. She was everything to me from as far back as I can remember, and I loved her beyond measure.

As for my dad, he was my biggest fan. He believed in me through everything, even when I did not believe in myself. He trusted my intuition, my judgment, and he somehow taught me to trust in it, too. Because of all this, I guess, I felt like I could always go to him with anything, and no matter how much he wanted to fix it for me, he somehow managed to help me feel loved and heard even while he stepped back and let me handle it.

The biggest example of this for me came when I was twenty-nine or thirty years old, had my own home, and lived alone. I wasn't married, and this bothered my dad, mostly because he thought I might be lonely. He'd come over for iced tea on my back porch and ask me again if I was lonely and again I would tell him I wasn't, I was just fine.

Then I met someone. And it moved so fast, I couldn't catch my breath, but no one commented on how fast it was moving because I think everyone thought it was high-time I got married anyway. And they wanted that for me, the good things of marriage, and I know my parents didn't want me to be alone anymore. He asked me to marry him six months after we met. This was in 1995, and we were engaged to be married in April.

But around January, I started feeling this heaviness in my gut, this uncertainty, something I couldn't label or say what it was. I called Dad—he was in Florida—and I told him I didn't know, I wasn't sure, I felt funny about the wedding. I wasn't sure I should be doing it, getting married.

And he told me, well, it was probably cold feet and he had it when he married Mom. He told me he pulled into a driveway on his way to marry Mom and just sat there in his car, wondering if he was doing the right thing. He told me it was pretty common, getting cold feet, and I really shouldn't worry about it.

Well, another month went by, and I still wasn't sure. I called Dad about three times when he was in Florida, and each time he talked me down. It was hard for me to know, because I was a little phobic about commitment, about getting married, and I had nothing to compare it to.

Fast-forward to April, and we have 250 people coming to our wedding from five different states, and it's one week before the wedding. My friends had a bachelorette party for me, I ended up spending the night at Mom and Dad's, and when I woke up the next morning, a week before my wedding, I started sobbing. I went up to the kitchen table and was just distraught.

I sat there and cried and told my parents I didn't know what I was doing, and I didn't think I should be getting married, and they both listened while I went on for a bit. I talked for two or three hours, and Dad started pacing around the house, and I could tell that Mom wasn't happy with me. I think she thought I was being ridiculous—I silently agreed with her.

After a couple of hours of this, Dad came over and sat down beside me. He stared deep into my eyes and he said, "Tammy, here's what we're going to do. You're going to get up from this table and go home. And you're going to come back here on Wednesday at five p.m., and I am going to have every family member here at the table, and you're going to show up with a final decision on this thing. If you're going to marry him, you're going to stop crying, and if you're going to back out, then we will undo this wedding."

Mom started freaking out at the thought.

"Jean," my dad said. "Everyone comes to the wedding for a party, but at the end of the night, they go home. Tammy is the one who has to go home and put her head on her own pillow. We're going to get this right."

Dad walked me out to the car and gave me a hug and we were both crying, and I knew in that moment he so badly wanted to fix it because he couldn't handle me being so upset. I wasn't normally the emotional girl, and he knew my distress was real.

He pulled away and before I got in the car, he said, "I can't do this for you, Tammy. You have to figure this out. I can't do it. The only thing I can do is support your decision. So, you go now, and you figure it out."

I worked in Harrisburg, so I had a couple of days of commuting to really think about what I was going to do. It was an awful couple of days. One moment I thought I had it right in my mind, the next moment I changed my mind completely. It was such a difficult decision. Anyway, I came to my conclusion and returned to my parents' house at five p.m. on Wednesday and sat down at the table with the entire family. Everyone's eyes were on me. This is the Wednesday before the Saturday of my wedding, and my fiancé didn't even know I was having these second thoughts.

I looked up at everyone, and I said, "I'm not going to do it. I'm not marrying him."

My dad didn't even hesitate. "Okay." He started handing out papers. "We have 250 people to call. You can do these seventy-five." He handed some to my sister. "And you can call these." He distributed information to each of my siblings.

He looked at me. "You're going to call the girls in your wedding party, and Jean, you're going to call off the reception— get it undone."

He had it all figured out, and by that point, Mom was on board. I had my three siblings sitting there beside me thinking, *This is ridiculous*. It was like we were little kids again, and Dad was telling us all what to do. And I didn't blame them. It felt ridiculous to me as well. The only thing that felt more ridiculous was the alternative.

But then Dad looked at me. "Tonight," he said. "Right now, you get in your car, drive to your fiancé's house, and tell him you're not going to marry him. Your sister is going with you."

No one spoke. He commanded the moment. My sister and I left, and everyone else did what he had assigned them to do.

That was one of the hardest things I ever had to do in my life.

But the whole point of this story isn't the decision I made—the point is that my dad became the Superstar Dad in that moment. How he knew what to do, I'll never know—he was a natural in these kinds of situations. I couldn't have asked for a better person to come alongside me in that moment.

Everything he had taught me in my entire life came together in that moment. I knew he had my best in mind, I knew he would do what he had to in order to care for me, and I knew he would stand with me, no matter what I decided. Everything he had communicated to me throughout my entire life was real, and he proved it there.

We got through it, and Dad never really brought it up to me again. Once it was over, it was over.

Fast-forward two-and-a-half years, and I married someone else, and I knew what I was doing, what I was getting into. I had my master's degree by then and my own home, and in that moment, again, my dad's support was huge.

When Dad is gone, I think what I'll miss the most is having my biggest fan right here with me. I've always had this sense, since I was a little girl, that Dad is my biggest fan. He is the one person on Earth who has always been right there at the forefront of my life, cheering me on. I have amazing, first-class girlfriends, no doubt, but there's something about my dad. Maybe it's just because he's my dad. I'll miss the times I will feel the need to call him and ask him his opinion or the times I want to share what's happening in my life. Every moment when I'm prompted to pick up the phone and call him after he's gone will be a hard moment.

One of my all-time favorite things about my dad is his unique sense of humor. It is different than most and I *love* it! He has made me laugh and smile so often throughout the years, and

I will miss that one day . . . a lot! We have an awesome connection as father and daughter, and I will forever be thankful to God for blessing me with Steve Fisher as my dad.

If I had to describe my dad in one word, it would probably be "consistent," although later in life, I'd choose the word "blessed." Yes, he's driven and enthusiastic, but he could never have done his life this well without the favor of God. As stated in Ephesians 3:20, "Glory to God who is able to do far beyond all that we could ask or imagine by His power at work within us."

Kurt

My mother, Jean Louise (Erb) Fisher, was the women behind the man, the backbone of our family, and without the "she," there wouldn't have been "we" or "he." She loved unconditionally, all of us kids and her husband. If I had one word to describe her it would be "passionate." She was always smiling, greeted everyone with open arms.

Who was she and where did she come from? To dig a little deeper, we must go back in time. Born June 17, 1936, she was the daughter of Walter and Arlene Erb, the oldest of five children, and she grew up in Pequea on River Road, not far from Pinnacle Point. Her grandparents were Cora (Sellers) Erb and Maris Erb. She went to a one-room schoolhouse with mostly cousins and local neighbors, while her father worked at the Holtwood Dam, dredging coal off the bottom of the riverbed from a barge. Later, he worked as a welder. Walt was strong as a bull and never broke a bone. They lived off the land and all worked hard.

My father met her at a roller-skating rink and later married her when she was only nineteen years old.

She was passionate about life, the Lord, her husband, her family, her friends, and her community. She was president of the school's PTA, a den mother in Cub Scouts, ran church events, and even ran for supervisor one year in local politics. She embraced anyone who entered her space and made them feel welcomed. All of this gave my father the opportunity to concentrate on the building of the business and then on the operation.

She always wanted to be a race-car driver and a PE teacher. I didn't know it growing up, but her favorite color was black. Still, I never remember any of her cars or much of anything being black.

She enjoyed sports and was my most devoted fan, coming to every baseball game, football game, wrestling match, running competition, boxing match, or gymnastic event that any of us ever had. Her voice was loud—I could always hear her cheering us on, as enthusiastic as if she was in the event herself.

It was during the 60s and 70s, when most women stayed home and took care of the home and the children. There was one car and usually one garage door. It was the time of milkmen and door-to-door salesmen. I remember her always letting the salesmen in but immediately telling them she wasn't buying anything they had to offer. She would let them do their demonstrations and afterward, sign on the dotted line. Not every one of them, but a good many benefitted from her engaged interest in whatever anyone else was willing to talk about.

Watching these interactions helped my career as a salesman later in life.

Our family was very regimented and had a good routine. Pop was up for his six a.m. shower and got my sisters up at 6:15. He would eat and be out the door before any of us children made it to the kitchen. Mother had breakfast ready and off to school we went. Dinner was five thirty p.m. sharp and you better not be late or Pop met you at the door.

For around fifteen years, on Friday nights, they left at six thirty p.m. to go bowling and returned at nine thirty sharp. Church was every Sunday, and we had many a Sunday brunch at the Historical Strasburg Inn (now Fireside). We also held our company's holiday parties there, with meals served family-style for all the employees and their entire families. It usually involved entertainment with Santa providing gifts for all.

My mother loved making ceramics and one year made every woman in the company (and wife of any employee) a set of angel candle holders. Their employees worked hard, and they showered them with love and appreciation. They grew corn and asparagus, which we children helped pick and distribute to the employees. They also held picnics on their farm in the 80s with gifts, clowns, games, and, of course, a dunk tank for the men to take out their frustrations on the boss.

One of my earliest memories is from when we lived at Rawlinsville. There was a hotel there on the corner, and every fall a lot of migrant workers came through because in those days people grew a lot of tomatoes on those farms, and they needed help bringing in the harvest. They'd bring in the wagon loads right there across from the post office, and tractor trailers would pull out of there full of green tomatoes. I remember seeing all of the different nationalities come through.

But Mother used to also pick tomatoes out there, I guess to make a little extra money, and one of the days we were out there, it was just so hot. Mom had a thermos, and she handed it to me and told me to take it and get her some water. I ran it over to the farmer's wife, and it was one of those old thermoses with the glass liner inside of it. The woman filled up the thermos, and I took off running to get this water to Mom, but I fell and shattered the inside. Thank goodness she didn't just pick it up and try to drink it, but I felt so bad because she was so thirsty. I went back up to the farmhouse and the lady gave me something else to fill with water.

Speaking of Mom, she treated everyone the same, whether they had a nickel or they had a million dollars. She was a real servant of the Lord in the way she helped everyone. Some of our friends, just teenagers having a hard time, lived with us for a year or two at a time. My parents took them in, and a lot of the reason for that was our mom—she had such a heart for people, helping people, and she was a good example to us in that.

As you know, Dad ended up welding, too, and the job he got rigging steel was no joke, but that's what he did. Back then, the rigger climbed up the steel without safety harnesses or anything like that. You just scaled up without a ladder. How do you get up? Right there. Climb up the beam. My brother and I did it, too, for a time.

When you're rigging steel, you carry around a belt with two spud wrenches, a big hammer that weighs two or three pounds, and a bag of bolts. You're probably carrying around forty pounds or so. You climb up the steel beam and stick the spud wrench in a hole, and then use that for your seat, staying there until the crane guy swings the beam around. You guide the beam in and then stick a bolt in it. Once your end is attached, the guy on the other end attaches his, and you walk across the beam to start the next one. And you do that all day long.

When you're shimmying up steel beams, carrying that kind of weight, guiding in beams and bolting things together, you're a rock. You're in the best shape of your life. It's not surprising that when Dad showed up for basic training, he was in amazing shape.

Because of Dad, I was welding when I was ten years old and could run every piece of equipment in the shop by the time I was twelve. Even when I was only six, Dad would have me in there chipping slag off the stick weld joints. When Dad got the job making rings for New Holland, these big skids were delivered to the shop full of these parts that needed to be welded together. He'd weld them, and I'd spend a few hours chipping the slag off.

All through our childhood, we worked half a day all summer long. And during the year, when we got off the bus, often he'd have blueprints for us to run—everyone needed a copy, and those old machines took forever to print, so we'd get off the bus and go down to the shop until dinner time. And every single Friday night, it was our job to sweep the shop. When I say "our" job, I mean me and Steve. And that place was immaculate. That was Dad's thing—everything needed to be clean and in order. He ran a tight ship that way.

Besides the shop, there were always chores to do when we got home. Dad always left a list. Lots of edging the grass and the flower beds and the driveway, and when Dad got home, you better

164

believe he was going to inspect your work. If it wasn't done right? You had to do it over again, from the beginning. If he told me to sweep out the garage, and I went quick because I wanted to go hang out with my friends, he'd come in after work and look around. "Why didn't you move stuff? Why'd you just sweep around that shelf? Why is it dirty in the corners?" And then I had to do it again. Take everything out and start from scratch. That's just how it was.

Do it right or don't bother doing it at all. It was a good lesson, and it's taken me a long way.

Just before we moved, Pop injured his leg playing softball. He had an operation to repair his torn knee ligament, and once we moved into the rancher on Breezy Knoll, he used to sit on the edge of the built-in butcher table and exercise his leg. He would take one of my mother's pocketbooks and put weight in it and flex his leg. After a few weeks, he had added so much weight that he cracked the table. I remember that crack being there for a long time

We had a great childhood. We didn't have to worry about friction between our parents—they almost never fought. They had sort of the typical Amish relationship, as far as that goes: Dad's job was to work and bring home the money, and Mom's job was to cook and take care of the house. But cooking was kind of a necessary evil for Mom—I don't think she loved it, and I can't say she was the best cook in the world. All the meals were meat and potatoes, plus a vegetable, stick it on the stove and stick it on high! Every once in a while, she'd burn something, and Dad would give her a hard time, but after I got older, I started sticking up for her, taking her side.

We didn't just work, though. We hunted and fished together, and I remember when I got my first big buck. I was about thirteen years old, and Dad and I were hunting right there behind our house in Willow Street. It was raining, wet, and cold, and we were getting close to the end of the day. Dad was pushing for me all day, really wanting me to get something, and it was harder in those days to find deer. There just weren't as many around as there are today. Anyway, we were sitting there and out comes this buck, running through the woods, and I put up my rifle and took a shot—it was a lucky shot, I'll admit. My gun jammed and everything. When we went down and found it, we both just sat there and cried—I was so happy, and he was happy for me.

Dad became really involved in skeet shooting. Which reminds me of another chore we did—we'd come home from school and load shotgun shells for Dad. I loaded thousands of those things in my childhood. He practiced twice a week and the guys would give him a hard time because we'd load them real fast and didn't always get the right measure of powder, so sometimes the shells would just go *Pop!* and the guys would laugh and say, "I see your boys have been loading your shells again, Steve."

We got to travel a lot, and he met a bunch of influential people through skeet shooting, traveling up and down the East coast. He shot in Puerto Rico just about every year, and we got to go there a few times, too.

When we lost Mother, it was hard on him. It was hard on all of us.

He's been a good father, very fair and honest. He doesn't make rash decisions. He's a processor, takes everything in, and thinks hard about it. When we kids got into little scrapes with each other, he would always think about things and take in everyone's perspectives.

He's also been really good at leaving the past in the past. Things that might be uncomfortable or things he doesn't want to dwell on, he's good at leaving that behind. That's one of the things he taught us early on, even when we were young—make decisions as a family, and as the business grows, money will never tear us apart. He treated everyone fair, and he was determined that the business would be something that was good for all of us.

He always told us it wasn't about the money—it was about the things we could do with the money. The money was just a tool, just an opportunity to do things a lot of people can't do. And we all ended up being part of the business at different times and in different ways. It's been good to us. Certainly, we've had some tough times, like any family business, but overall, it's been good to us.

It wasn't just we kids who respected Dad. Even though he was only five-six, he walked with confidence and wasn't afraid of anyone. He used to go into the city and collect rent from these huge guys, and sometimes I'd go in with him. I could tell these guys were scared of my dad. He came for his money and he expected to get the rent. Sometimes there would be a note that he should come down to the bar to get the rent, and he'd go down, collect the rent, and then buy a round of drinks for everyone.

He was a good leader, and during that time when we had 125 employees, they were all loyal because my parents treated them like family. Mom and Dad were good at recognizing and appreciating the work people did for them.

When I think of Dad, one word that comes to mind is "focused." Even when he was out skeet shooting, he was mentally tough and could really focus on the task at hand, just that thing right in front of him.

He was a good dad, and I learned a lot from him.

Patti

When I was little and we lived in Rawlinsville, our phone was on a party line. I don't know how many people shared the same line, but when you'd dial, you'd only dial the last four numbers, then pick up the phone and make sure no one was on it. Sometimes, I'd listen in if someone was having a conversation. It was a fun house to live in, and I have a few fun memories of Dad from that house.

Like the time he bought Steve and me new Schwinn bikes. Steve's was red and mine was blue. But then one day after I finished riding it, I left it in front of the garage door and it got run over. I was devastated, but Dad was very matter-of-fact about it— I hadn't taken care of it, and that's what happens when you don't take care of your things.

I think we lived in Rawlinsville when Dad started going

hunting out west, and one time when he returned home, he brought me a cowgirl suit with white cowgirl boots and a white cowgirl hat. Each of the boys got suits and hats, too, and I just loved it. Every pair of boots he got me were white and pointy, and I wore them out. I so badly wanted to be a cowgirl because I loved horses. Now, here I am, the owner of a ranch, and I wonder how much of that is because of Dad buying me those cowgirl outfits when I was little.

We moved to Willow Street when I was eight years old, and when that house was being built, Dad would take us up there a lot. We'd sit in it while it was being framed and listen to music playing through the intercom he had installed. I think we'd go up there, not because he had anything he needed to do, but just because he wanted to soak it all in—that house was a dream come true for him. It was a beautiful ranch home, all stone, and the culmination of all of his hard work up to that point. We went up there a lot and just walked around inside of it while it was being built.

It was at that house on Willow Street where he returned from a big hunting trip with moose horns on top of our Comet station wagon—they were too big to fit inside the car.

Dad was always curious about how things were built, but especially anything that had a steel frame, so when the bridge in Holtwood was being constructed, he'd often drive all of us down there after church on a Sunday and watch the bridge go up. We'd sit in the car, and he'd get out and walk all around it, looking at it from different angles. He was fascinated with it, how it was coming together.

Then came the shop in Willow Street—when he bought

that, it was small and had a Coke machine out front. Back then, there were a few neighborhood kids who would hang out at the Coke machine, and sometimes they'd steal sodas. But Dad didn't chase them off or call the cops—he put them to work. He put a lot of teenage boys to work back then, a lot of them, and some of them worked hard and some didn't, but he was always trying to mentor them or teach them something or get them going in a good direction. And Mom was from Holtwood, so he hired boys from there, too. Sometimes they worked out and sometimes they didn't, but there was something in Dad that always wanted to give everyone a chance.

I guess I was about ten years old when I started cleaning the offices every Friday night—vacuuming the carpets and dusting and waxing the floors. After they were waxed, I had to buff them with one of those big machines. And I also had to clean the disgusting bathrooms, including the men's room, and those guys would always put their cigarette butts in the urinals. Well, I'd write little notes and put them above the urinals: "Stop throwing your butts in the urinals!" I was only ten or eleven at the time, and the men would usually draw pictures all over my notes. And they kept throwing their butts in the toilets. I can't believe I had to clean that disgusting place.

Meanwhile, Steve and Kurt were out doing stuff in the shop—welding or grinding or sweeping shop. And I was cleaning. And you have no idea how many times Dad would come inside and look at my work, shake his head, and tell me to do it again. It wasn't good enough. Often that meant I had to go back the next day, Saturday, and do a better job.

We also ran a lot of blueprints. The copier machine was

huge, and there was this little bottle of pure ammonia that I had to flip the bottle up and run the prints. It smelled so strong. We ran tons of those prints for the detailing department.

Dad hired a secretary when I was around thirteen or fourteen years old. Her name was Carol Davis, and she was the foreman's daughter, straight out of high school. I started working with her in the office, and soon after she arrived, I started going to school only half days and then working in the office the other half of the day, keeping the general ledger by hand, doing the books, the payroll, everything. Soon after that, when I was nineteen, I had a baby, so I did the payroll at home for quite a few years and learned that system.

During those years, I was with Dad every day, half a day, and I saw firsthand that he was really good to his employees. He had a lot of respect for them. And he wore a suit and tie every single day he went into the office, always looked nice. He was also a talented delegator, trusting people to do the job right.

You know, he trusted us kids, too. Whenever we asked him about something, he'd say the same thing: "You can do it. Figure it out." My whole life, that's what I got. He says the same thing to this very day—if I go to him with a question, he'll say, "You can figure it out."

We learned to figure it out.

I went and got a job at Y&S Candies, in the licorice factory, and I was pretty proud about that because it was the first job I got outside of Dad. I had never worked for anyone else. For two years I worked there, and then I got a job at the post office, but when you started there, they started you part time, so I went back and worked for Dad. I figured I could do that until the post office was ready to take me on full time. I got into the contracts and negotiating, learned how to use the computers. Things had changed.

Dad knew my plan was to eventually go back to the post office, so he came to me one day and said he wanted me there, in his company. He wanted me to come back full time, and I told him, okay, that worked for me, but I got paid good money at the post office so he'd have to negotiate with me. We negotiated, and he brought me back full time to work for him.

Initially I was in purchasing. And I liked it. When I was twenty-six, he called me into his office. He had recently built that new fabrication shop across the street—this would have been around 1987 or 1988—and they were still working the bugs out. He told me he was going to start a new company in the old building that would do miscellaneous metal work.

"And you're going to run it," he told me.

"I don't how to do that! I don't even know how to read a blueprint. I know all the office stuff, but I don't know the operation."

"Figure it out," he said. "Your start date is October 1, 1988. Hire your people, form your corporation. Figure it out."

"What?" I asked, still unsure.

"Don't worry. We'll help you."

Well, I had no help. None. I had to form the corporation, learn about steel fabrication, pick the new name, and hire a graphic designer for the log. I even took welding lessons and blueprint reading lessons and learned how to do some estimating. Dad sold me the equipment in that building, and we had a lease agreement. I hired employees. And I started on October 1, 1988. I was president for thirteen years.

The timing was rough for Dad, though, taking on all of that debt and moving into a bigger building at the height of a recession. If he would have stayed in the building he sold to me, he would have done fine. But while his business struggled, we were able to use the new business to help through some of those tough years. It all worked out.

After that, my brothers came over to this new company, and I kind of put my foot on the brakes a lot while they were pushing for growth. So, Dad stepped in again as the mediator when there were things we couldn't agree on, and he would sit down with us and help us figure it out.

It was hard because, growing up, I was the difficult one. I was the one who didn't always make good choices. In fact, when he had me run Steel Fab, I think it was after about a year that he walked in while I was working on blue prints and apologized for not identifying my strengths sooner. Evidently, he hadn't always believed in me—he would tell me, go do it, but in his heart, he didn't believe it. But he told me that day that I had a lot to offer, and that was a really big deal. It meant a lot to me.

It was really hard when Mom died. I took care of her for the last six weeks. She told me, when she died, that Dad would remarry because he didn't like being alone, and I didn't want to hear that. I was pretty upset when women started calling him a few months after Mom died. I told him not to call any of them back because Mom was barely gone! But I guess he found it flattering.

If I had to describe my dad in one word, it would be "strong." Very strong—strong-willed, mentally strong, physically strong. I still see him as a very strong man.

I've been totally blessed with my mom and dad—I had a great mom and dad, and I don't think there are a lot of people who can say that.

When Dad's gone, I think the thing I'll miss the most about him is his advice, his wisdom. He has a lot of wisdom, and he has always shared it freely.

I wouldn't trade my dad for the world.

Steve

My dad is a guy who grew up in a time in history when things weren't easy, and not just for his family—for a lot of families. It molded him to be who he was. He learned to work hard, coming from the Amish. All of his brothers and sisters worked hard. I guess we all learn from our upbringing, all of us learn subconsciously about how we think things should be. I just feel completely blessed that I had two parents who stayed together and who worked together. My father came from nothing, and he accomplished a lot. He's a hard-working guy, always has been.

The earliest memories I have of Dad are of him working. A lot. I knew, even at a young age, that he was working hard all the time. He would come home so tired, he'd flop back in the easy chair and say, "Could someone please take off my shoes for me?" That's my earliest memory of him. Sometimes they were laced up so tight we could barely get his shoes off. Sometimes it was a challenge just getting those laces untied. But we would, and we'd pull and pull until they came off.

I don't feel like I saw him a lot when I was a kid, apart from in the evenings—he had his own business and he'd often work after dinner. Some of my favorite times during those years came when we went hunting together. He went out with me, and I took an interest in it. Those were really cool times.

And he did always try to take us somewhere on vacation— even though having his own business meant he had to work harder than most people, it also meant he had more freedom. He would take us places and give us a chance to try different things— we'd go up into the mountains for a week or go to this place called Lake Harmony where they had canoes. We went up there for several years, and it was a lot of fun.

Once I got out of school, I came to work for him. I worked in the field for two or three years and then moved into the office, which meant I saw him all the time. You know, in those early years, I didn't realize how blessed I was, having that time with my father. It was good. We worked hard, and we tried to make the business successful. I was there helping, and it felt good to help my dad, and eventually my brother Kurt came on, after he got out of college. Later Patti came into the business, and later down the road, Tammy got involved.

Having a family business was good—it was always his dream to have that.

He still works hard. He's eighty-nine years old and he comes over here every morning at five a.m., and he walks around in the shop trying to find things he can do to make it better. He still wants to work. He still wants to help. He might be eighty-nine, but he has more energy than I do. I can't understand it.

When I grow up, someday, I want to be like him.

If I had to describe my dad in one word, I'd say "driven." He's driven in everything he does, but he's also conscientious about it. He never does it halfway, never cuts corners, never cheats anyone. But he's driven. Whether it's been in his steel business or in his hobbies like skeet shooting, he wanted to be the best.

There was a time when he was younger and just a bit sharper when he was considered one of the best skeet shooters in Pennsylvania. For many years, he was one of the best. They used to have this thing where they would take the five best skeet shooters in every state and put them up against shooters in other states, and they'd compete in Puerto Rico. There were some years the Pennsylvania team he was on won the whole thing. Dad was really good with a .410, a small gauge shotgun, and he hit 100 straight targets with a .410 when not many people were doing that.

I used to go along and shoot skeet some, too, but I was just never as good at it as he was. I could never shoot 100 straight. I tried it and I just didn't have the natural ability or whatever it takes. It was cool, though, because he took me along and registered me to shoot in the junior division. I did that in my early teens for a few years, and it was always fun getting to spend time with my dad.

Of course, you talk about Dad and you have to talk about Mom, too. They were such a great team. They worked so well together. My mother was a stay-at-home mom, a housewife, and she took care of the house—that was her domain. She washed our clothes, made us meals, took care of the house, and every day she'd take the list of chores my dad wrote up and make sure we did them all before he got home from work. So, she had to manage us and our chores and the house. It was quite an undertaking. She also paid all the bills, took care of the shopping, and knew where we were at, financially. She was very frugal, and she was a good manager of the house. She always knew where to find deals and how to stretch a dollar.

I guess that's what I mean by them being a great team—Dad worked hard and made the money, and Mom stretched that money and made it go far. She was a great mom, always happy, always laughing. Of course, if you didn't do what you were supposed to do, she could get tough. And it was always warranted, when she did. We needed that a lot.

Those chores—we worked hard and we played hard. My dad had to work hard growing up, and so that list he gave us was never a short one. Sometimes Kurt and I would get a little ticked about how much work he left us to do after school. The girls helped mom inside, so Kurt and I took care of the yard, all the outside stuff, and we had to keep the wood box filled up. Dad burned a lot of wood. We split it all with axes and wedges, and sometimes our after-school chores took us an hour or so before we were free to go do other things. Sometimes our friends got tired of waiting for us and helped us get our chores done.

There's one story about my dad that always makes me smile. He's always been extremely competitive, and whether it be with the business or with skeet shooting or hunting, he always wanted to be the best. Anyway, in his later years, when he couldn't skeet shoot as well as he used to, he decided to take up golfing.

He played a lot with my father-in-law, Clayton Frackman,

and that's something else I feel blessed about—he and my father-in-law have always gotten along well. One year, they got into a shoot-out between the two of them at one of the local club's senior tournaments. Just the two of them left, so they had to go one hole at a time until one of them won a hole, and that person would win the whole tournament. One of them was going to win, and they're both competitive, and they like to rib each other about it.

It was neck and neck, and they even had people following them around the course to see who would win, like in the PGA. They got up to a par three, and my dad hit his tee shot to within a few feet of the hole. It was a great shot. He knew it would probably win him the tournament.

Well, my father-in-law stopped him and said something like, "Fisher, you're going to have to rehit that ball. Look where your tee is." He pointed out that my dad's tee was in front of the stakes in the tee box. Well, Dad wasn't into that, and he said he wasn't going to. My father-in-law said, "Fine, we'll just talk to the official about it when we get back to the clubhouse."

I guess my dad conceded and took another shot, this time landing about twenty feet from the pin. When my father-in-law first told me this story, he looked at me and smiled. "What do you think your dad said to me, while we were walking down to that green? He looked at me and said, 'How's it feel to be an asshole?' Can you believe that? Can you hear your dad saying that to me?"

They tied that hole, went on, and eventually my dad made an unbelievable putt to win the match. But that story always makes me laugh, because I can just about hear my dad asking that question.

What will I miss most about Dad when he's gone? I think just having him. He's one of my best friends. Every day I have him here is a blessing. Every day he comes to the office—I love it when he comes in. He'll come sit in my office and tell me what's going on in the shop and after we chat for a little, he's like, "Let's go get some lunch."

Every day that I get to take him out and buy him lunch, it's a blessing. I can talk to him about anything. And he can talk to me about anything. I'm going to miss that.

Steve Fisher Answers a Few Questions

1.   What do you know for sure? What has life taught you?

I've been around for nine decades. One thing I know is that
when life hands you lemons, you have to make lemonade. I also
know that I'm a determined individual, and I've had to count on
my determination to get me through. Also, when God puts the
right person in your life, it changes everything—whether that
was Jean who showed me what true affection is or other people
who opened doors for me in the business world along the way,
which happened many times in my life.

2.   Do you have any regrets?

You know, I can't think of any. Not really. There could have been, if I'd have pursued some things a little further. But I have no regrets.

3. Who was the person who impacted the course of your life the most?

I have to say, my wife Jean. By all means, she was the most important person in my life. Up until the time I met her, I was a little lost in the world, didn't know which way I was going. I just can't say enough about her. She was the guardian angel on my shoulder from then on, along with God. Getting to know her was magical, and she was the perfect match for me. I needed a woman with a bit of a backbone, because I could be a bit of a bully sometimes, but she was so supportive and wonderful, loving, and fun. That was Jean.

4. What was the most beautiful place you ever visited?

The tundra. I spent ten days there, which was just absolutely amazing. They have six weeks of summer up there, and I went the second week of July, right in the middle of the summer season, and during that time the ice is all melted off the tundra and everything is lakes. You could take a shovel and drive it down about eight inches to solid ice. We were there ten days, and it never got completely dark. We had our sleeping bags and crawled in and slept on the ground, and when we woke up in the morning, it would change from the time we went to bed, with flowers covering the tundra. I never saw anything like it. Also, the sun and the moon are so much brighter. There's no light pollution. Everything is bright as can be. It's a little like Montana—they have the brightest stars you've ever seen. When I was a child, that's how our skies were here in Lancaster. I was with Harry Stilwell and the pilot who flew us there—we went up in a pontoon plane that landed in the lake from Cambridge Bay to Victoria Bay, and we lived on Arctic Char for ten days. When the sun went down, it got cooler, maybe around 45 degrees, but when it came back up, it reached about 70.

5. What is your favorite . . .

Animal? A dog. I don't have one now, but I do love dogs. I trained beagles for our rabbit and pheasant hunting, and I loved those little pups. They have a great sense of smell, and I'd take Jean out in the evening when the puppies were developing and they'd yip at the rabbits, but they wouldn't go very far. That was really fun, training beagles.

Athlete? Joe Namath, the quarterback of the Jets. He won the Super Bowl in New York, and from then on, I followed him until he retired. Broadway Joe.

Card game? Gin Rummy. I started playing in the service. Pinochle, gin, chess. We had nothing but time in the evenings. I still play regularly with my best friend, Dave Anderson. He's a man of few words, but when he says something, you listen.

Candy? Candy-coated peanuts or Good&Plenty.

Holiday? Christmas. Christmas when I was a boy meant getting an orange and peanuts, but when I got married to Jean, she loved Christmas so much. I put my shoe outside the fireplace, sprinkled ashes around it, and then took away the shoe and made it looked like a footprint. The kids thought it was Santa. Jean made Christmas magical.

Cookie? Chocolate chip, a little on the burnt side. When I chew on something, I want to know I'm chewing on something. So now Rosene makes me a few burnt ones, whenever she makes cookies.

Color? Green. The car was green, the kitchen was green. The shutters were green. That was always my favorite color.

Drink? Margarita on the rocks with salt.

Famous Person? Donald Trump. I think he is the greatest guy. I liked him long before he was president. He wrote a book twenty-five or thirty years ago, *The Art of the Deal*, and after I read that, I said, "This guy would make a good president."

Season? I like the winter because I can live in Florida. We've been going there for many, many years. I enjoy Florida in the winter time. In Lancaster, the four seasons are just great. Fall is my favorite in PA, the most beautiful time, when the leaves are changing. Jean and I used to take a trip up through New England when the leaves were at their peak.

Sport? Skeet shooting, hunting, fishing, and football. I love all of those in my life. When I started making money I was able to do the things I could never do before, and I worked hard just to be able to do that. I could remember when I was a boy, we had a day a year when the Amish went fishing, Ascension Day. I wanted my dad to go with me, but he never did. Fly Fishing and trapping in my younger life were amazing. My football team is the Philadelphia Eagles.

Ice Cream? Butter pecan.

6. What was the hardest choice you had to make in your life?

Leaving my family at sixteen years old, that was hard. Leaving the Amish faith and my family. That was very, very hard. I had a family of thirteen siblings and walked away from that, not knowing when I'd get back, if I ever would, and knowing I wouldn't get help if I needed it. That was tough.

7. What is the secret to a happy marriage?

First of all, 50/50. You have to compromise to the point that you feel you're giving 50 percent to the other person. Jean had patience with me. Jean was such a positive person, and if she had something to say, she'd tell me.

8. Is there anything you wanted to do that you did not get

around to doing? In other words, is there anything left on your "Bucket List?"

I wanted to jump out of an airplane. Not by myself. Tandem. I always thought I'd like to do that.

9. Do you have any advice on how to bounce back after hard times?

There were many times in my life that things weren't going well. I wondered if I would make it or have to go back and work for a paycheck instead of owning my own business. Those thoughts came into my mind a few times during tough decisions. Sheer determination is a good way to explain how I got through.

Two steps forward, one back. I went through that quite a bit. I didn't have anyone to go to, had to work it out myself. I didn't even know how to figure out the overhead of my business until later, when the kids went to school and came back and brought that into the company. I had no education, had to figure out things that were tough, things that you go to school to learn.

Get back up. I had to get back up a lot. I didn't see any other options.

10. What was the most important invention of your lifetime?

Something that intrigued me in my life was when engineers first built these big 727 passenger planes that held 200 people. I thought that was amazing, watching them go up in the air.

Then there was the calculator. We were doing everything manually, and then they created this thing that came up with the answer and spit it out on a piece of paper. The first one I bought was sixty pounds and cost $1,000. It was this huge, clunky thing, the most amazing piece of machinery. No time later, they made tiny ones that fit in your pocket.

Of course, then there was the fax machine. When that came out, I thought it was the greatest thing since the wheel. We could put out bids and ask sub-contractors to give us a price on various things, and you'd go home and sleep and the next morning the answer was on the fax machine, instead of taking two to three days. That was a real turning point in communication between sub-contractors and us.

And when computers first came out, I had someone come in and built one for us. It cost $25,000. After that was finally finished and we started using it, it was outdated. That's how fast they advanced.

11. What was the biggest piece of equipment you ever purchased?

I was in the business to the point where everything we were doing, we were doing well, and we were ready for an advance in the business. I felt as though in order to go to the next level, I needed a crane, so I bought one in preparation to build the business bigger and more successful. And it really worked for me. We ended up with one crane, and following that, I had a fleet of cranes that we rented out and used ourselves. That first crane was a fifteen-ton. I got that around 1972, right after I bought the farm across the road. We had room to grow, and I thought a crane was part of that. By 1974, when we did the courthouse, I bought a big ninety-ton crane for that job.

When the company changed hands, they sold the cranes at the sale.

12. What are you the most thankful for in your life?

That I have four awesome children. I'm very fortunate to have four good kids, because at my age, well, you couldn't appreciate them any more than I do.

I'm thankful I've had two good wives with different personalities. They were very different people, but they are both good ladies.

I'm thankful for the fact that I was born into a challenge. God gave me a challenge in my life. I was born into this tough deal with a lot of siblings and a dad who didn't communicate and this basic Amish lifestyle, but this created or sparked in me a deep desire to overcome, to use it to my advantage. If I wasn't born into a challenge, maybe I wouldn't have accomplished so much in my life.

A part of that challenge came after I left the Amish and got out into the world and saw the opportunities that could be had. I never had any money growing up, but when I saw the opportunity of what money could do for you, I loved the challenge of making money. I saw that challenge and went after it. I am who I am because I started where I started.

This book was written, organized, and published with the help of Shawn Smucker. If you'd like to explore the possibility of having a book made about your family or loved one, you can reach Shawn at smucker.shawn@gmail.com or call 703-999-4079.